WINTER WELLNESS

In memory of Kalina Palka, who taught me how to build the perfect fire and shared her garden with me for a full year so I could grow my own Christmas dinner. Bright sparks shine on.

Dedicated to Sara Haglund, my foraging and fermenting friend. The first dandelion to open, pulling winter into spring.

Janus

Knowing new growth is near
but we are not yet met with its presence.
Instead, the bitter cold doth leave a prick upon your nose.
Time caught as a frosty layer coats the ground of years before.

Our marker of time tells us we do progress.
As we stray further from the joyous past we long.
Although it is a cycle, its chains are unoiled and in this month,
time does not provide us a stable journey, its pace not constant.

So, I beckon new growth to come,
when winter's over and spring's begun.

by Rory Gibson

RACHEL DE THAMPLE

WINTER
WELLNESS

*Nourishing recipes
to keep you healthy when it's cold*

BLOOMSBURY PUBLISHING
LONDON • OXFORD • NEW YORK • NEW DELHI • SYDNEY

FOREWORD BY
HUGH FEARNLEY-WHITTINGSTALL

The seasons are powerful forces that shape nature, and the rhythms of all life. If we think that doesn't include us, that we can step outside this cycle by cocooning ourselves in our over-heated, brightly lit buildings, we are making a mistake.

Our circadian, seasonal patterns of wakefulness and sleep, our flows of energy and the call for rest, have been forged within us over many millennia. They are more formative of our essential being than the modern world, which we have made in the blink of a restless eye. Embracing the seasons, then, is a wise move for our wellbeing, and essential if we are to draw on the full goodness that nature and careful cultivation can provide for our sustenance. A seasonal kitchen is a healthy and happy kitchen.

Yet, in winter especially, our busy lives urge us to resist the ancient messages that the shorter days, cooler temperatures and decreasing angles of the Sun's rays are activating within us: rest more, walk a little more slowly (and don't miss opportunities to connect with the beauty of the frost-tinged, low-lit, bare-branched landscape). Above all, replenish.

But true hibernation eludes us, and the pressure to keep up the pace when we should be slowing down makes us vulnerable. So feeding ourselves and our loved ones with nourishing food drawn from the wintry fields, as well as some saved and stored from the bounty of summer sunshine, is more vital than ever.

There is no one better to guide us through the opportunities to eat well and stay well in winter than the remarkable Rachel de Thample. Rachel has a deep knowledge of the power of good food to keep us in great shape. She understands the balance of nurture and nourishment with appetite and relish, the desire to delight the palate and let the soul soar, as well as the need to give the body all that it asks for.

Her palette is broad and full of goodness: potent seeds and grains, creamy roots and pillowy pulses, bittersweet winter leaves and punchy alliums, a wide spectrum of healing herbs and whole spices, an occasional thoughtful offering of respectfully chosen fish or meat. Rachel is also skilled in the techniques that harness and develop the potency of good ingredients for healing and restoration. Her ferments and broths, tonics and tisanes are treats in the true and often forgotten sense of the word: they treat us well.

Her words are as well-chosen as her ingredients, and her recipes sing with the promise of rich flavours, cultural adventures and sheer zest for life. Who wouldn't want to start the day with a Woodstock frying pan granola, or a Kimchi bokkeumbap, or sit down to a supper of Lemon-barley avgolemono, Mushroom mujaddara, or Coconut creamed kale aloo? And who could resist Rachel's Rooty rumbledethumps? Not me!

The mirage of a perpetual summer is seductive, but just as day needs night, the year needs winter to come full circle, for nature – and humanity – to replenish and recover. In the short days of the coldest season, it's valuable to take a breath from the churn of modern life. Just as we need sleep at night, we need rest in winter.

Our resistance to winter is spurred by the hum of our 24-hour society, which drives us to keeping moving against nature's will. We might not be designed to retreat into a full hibernating slumber when the Sun is shy, but our bodies – in the same way as plants – crave a period of dormancy... or at least a little slowing of the pace. Wellness, in all respects, springs from winter's rest.

This book is a cordial invitation for you to embrace the essential transition of a winter wind-down. It offers a replenishing repertoire of culinary treasures to both seduce the taste buds and fortify the immune system when we need it most, without sweating it out in the kitchen. Food is the delicious and nourishing bridge that connects us to both the Sun and the soil.

Heeding the 'Let food be thy medicine' philosophy, I've uncovered a trove of remedies, some dusted off from centuries ago and polished with a laid-back, modern touch. I've shone a light on delightful seasonal traditions and recipes from around the world that embrace the importance of winter's role in the seasonal calendar, offering nourishment on a deeper level.

Woven through the fabric of the book are notes on ingredients that shine brightest in winter – such as shellfish and citrus – the cold teasing out their sweetness. I've also looked at preserving traditions aligned with the frosty months, such as miso-making, or *kvass* for Christmas *barshch*, all tailored to invigorate you while delivering punchy flavours along with gut health. And with winter rest firmly in mind, recipes for foods and drinks that will help to ease you into a dreamy slumber are also threaded through these pages.

Harnessing the power of good food doesn't have to involve hours of prep, expensive ingredients or mile-long shopping lists. Some of the richest ingredients can be found for free, such as dandelions, elderberries or pine needles. We've lost connection with these highly nutritious foods because they are not sold in supermarkets and thus they've become unfamiliar. There's so much ancient wisdom around food that we've mislaid and so many traditions, too. I hope this book can help you begin to reclaim them.

Winter is delicious and essential. Its sting is not so sharp. We need it to reflect and rejuvenate. It is, after all, the season that bridges the old with the new. The season where the end meets the beginning.

FOOD AS MEDICINE

Just as we have lost connection with the rhythm of the seasons, there seems to be a disconnect of our minds from our bodies, how they work and what they need to thrive. The beauty of being empowered by this knowledge is that you are more in control when illness strikes. The brilliant news is that many ailments can be remedied, or at least eased, by delicious food.

All the recipes in this book are tailored towards bolstering both our immune and digestive systems, with gut health at the fore. We are coming to realise that a thriving microbiome is the epicentre of good health, helping us fight seasonal bugs and supporting long-term overall wellness.

Supporting our lungs is also important to help us fight infection, especially winter colds and flu, and luckily there are plenty of very appetising tools, such as ginger and horseradish, to help reinforce this vital organ. The skin – our largest organ – can also help us fight bad bugs. Bone broth, turmeric, dark leafy greens, olive oil, wheatgrass and fermented dairy such as kefir feed the skin, strengthening its ability to release bacteria-fighting oils.

What makes us ill...

No matter what the season, our immune systems are constantly challenged by pollutants in the air, the water and even the building materials in our homes. Nourishing the body with a wide variety of simple seasonal foods is the best way to help keep it strong and happy. We get ill when the normal workings of the body are disturbed. This can happen when a bacterium or virus enters the body, or because of unhealthy living practices such as lack of exercise, intake of drugs, or excessive sugar, salt and processed foods. Basically, when we move away from nature, our bodies suffer.

... and what can cure us

Returning to nature might help us heal. During the cold months, what we eat can, indeed, be our medicine. I've thought about this deeply while writing this book and devised the list below, which I hope will help you through the winter.

ARTHRITIS AND INFLAMMATION

HELPFUL INGREDIENTS almonds, bone broth, dark leafy greens, fish, ginger, kale, lemon, olive oil, turmeric, walnuts and walnut oil.
RECIPES Lemon-barley avgolemono, Golden butter (see pages 134 and 212).

BLOOD SUGAR AND DIABETES

HELPFUL INGREDIENTS bananas, buckwheat, eggs, fermented dairy, nuts, seeds.
RECIPES Overnight five seed bread, Probiotic ranch dressing, Digestive dukkah (see pages 40, 204 and 226).

CONCENTRATION AND FOCUS

HELPFUL INGREDIENTS *brahmi* (see page 49), broccoli, chia seeds, eggs, elderberries, nutmeg, oily fish, rosemary, spinach, sweet potatoes, walnuts.
RECIPES Celeriac tacos with kimchi and smoked mackerel, Spiced tahini cocoa (see pages 164 and 294).

COUGHS AND SORE THROATS

HELPFUL INGREDIENTS elderberry, honey, lemon, rosemary, thyme.
RECIPES Parsnip toddy, Apple scraps chai (see pages 132 and 272).

DETOXING

HELPFUL INGREDIENTS celeriac, celery, coriander, dandelion, wheatgrass.
RECIPES Celeriac Seville ceviche, Steamy dandelion oat latte (see pages 74 and 296).

DIGESTION AND GUT HEALTH

HELPFUL INGREDIENTS apples, apple cider vinegar, bone broth, coriander, cumin, dark leafy greens, fennel, ginger, ground flaxseed, kefir, mint, oats, olive oil, oregano, pumpkin seeds, sauerkraut.
RECIPES Boosted Bircher bowl, Levantine garlic paste (see pages 50 and 216).

ENERGY

HELPFUL INGREDIENTS almond milk, bananas, brown rice, coconut, dark leafy greens, ginger, matcha, pumpkin, sweet potatoes, turmeric.
RECIPES Banana bread blinis, Instant energising green soup (see pages 26 and 122).

FEVER AND FLU

HELPFUL INGREDIENTS carrots, chilli, garlic, ginger, honey, lemon, onions, oregano, rosemary, sage, thyme.
RECIPES Cough remedy carrots, Medicinal Chinese chicken soup (see pages 80 and 124).

HANGOVERS

HELPFUL INGREDIENTS bananas, *camu camu* (see page 48), dark leafy greens, eggs, ginger, olive oil, pumpkin seeds, red ginseng, wheatgrass.
RECIPES Kimchi bokkeumbap, Banana split (see pages 52 and 254).

HEADACHES

HELPFUL INGREDIENTS bone broth, ginger, lavender, lemon, mint.
RECIPES Rhubarb pickled ginger, Dandelion and burdock ramen (see pages 190 and 110).

HEART HEALTH

HELPFUL INGREDIENTS beetroot, buckwheat, chilli, hawthorn berries, pomegranate.
RECIPES Apple almond scones, Persian pomegranate poulet (see pages 42 and 175).

HORMONE HEALTH

HELPFUL INGREDIENTS flaxseed, *maca* (see page 49), miso, sage, sesame seeds.
RECIPES Carrot misozuke, Maple miso roast cauliflower, Paris tahini biscuits (see pages 192, 82 and 244).

IMMUNE SYSTEM HEALTH

HELPFUL INGREDIENTS   all citrus, bone broth, *camu camu* (see page 48), carrots, leafy greens, oysters, pumpkin seeds, squash, sweet potatoes.
RECIPES   Roast squash with kimchi butter, The Count's first negroni (see pages 96 and 282).

IRON BOOSTING

HELPFUL INGREDIENTS   beef, beetroot, chicken, dark leafy greens paired with citrus, dates, eggs, spirulina, sprouted pulses (see page 66).
Note: eat vitamin C-rich foods with greens and protein to aid iron absorption, and avoid consuming caffeine or calcium with them, for the same reason.
RECIPES   Winter spa smoothies, Wild and sprouted falafel with cardamom-lime tahini, Kimchi brisket stew (see pages 46, 64 and 143).

MENSTRUAL CRAMPS

HELPFUL INGREDIENTS   ginger, rose, saffron, *shatavari* (see page 49), turmeric.
RECIPES   Eshkeneh: Persian penicillin, Roasted rhubarb cranachan (see pages 128 and 238).

PROTEIN BOOSTING

HELPFUL INGREDIENTS   beef, buckwheat, chicken, fish, hemp seeds, lamb, miso, nuts, seeds.
RECIPES   Mushroom miso porridge, A lamb stew 'prescription' (see pages 34 and 180).

RELAXATION AND REDUCING ANXIETY

HELPFUL INGREDIENTS   *ashwagandha* (see page 49), bay, holy basil, lavender.
RECIPES   Bay-roasted beets, Four thieves vinegar, Holy basil chai (see pages 88, 202 and 295).

SKIN HEALTH

HELPFUL INGREDIENTS   bone broth, dark leafy greens, ginger, kefir, olive oil, turmeric, wheatgrass.
RECIPES   Turkish tahini greens, Turmeric and black pepper vinegar, Goji ginger tea (see pages 92, 200 and 274).

SLEEP

HELPFUL INGREDIENTS   bone broth, chamomile, cherry juice, lavender, lemon verbena, nutmeg, oats.
RECIPES   Carrot cake flapjacks, Chamomile Chardonnay, Night nog (see pages 32, 286 and 292).

SLOW AGEING

HELPFUL INGREDIENTS   bone broth, broccoli, dark leafy greens, goji berries, wheatgrass.
RECIPES   Wheatgrass, Broccoli bravas (see pages 31 and 160).

UPSET STOMACHS

HELPFUL INGREDIENTS   bone broth, fennel, ginger, liquorice, star anise.
RECIPES   Rise and shine tisane, Ginger biscuits (see pages 18 and 240).

BREAKFAST
AND
BRUNCH

When embraced with open arms,
winter can keep us warm.

*'To appreciate the beauty
of a snowflake it is necessary
to stand out in the cold.'*

Aristotle

In Norway, the concept of *koselig* is a secret of sorts. The idea is to celebrate the alchemy stirred by the chill in the air. This notion of winter has the breath of magic: it is the winter that brings the sparkle to morning's ice-speckled pavements, the winter of hazy lances of early sunshine dancing warmth through naked trees. The beauties of the coldest season are recognised by all nations. Those crepuscular rays at dawn – like breathy arrows piercing through a frosty forest – actually have a name in Japanese: *komorebi*.

We may feel further from the Sun in winter, but that is not the case. In truth, as we ebb into January, we're geographically closer to our pivotal star than at any other time of the year. A shift in the Earth's tilt is what defines the seasons, each of them a chapter framed by a solstice and an equinox. In summer, the Earth's slant allows more direct sun rays to kiss the Earth's surface, while in winter, the Sun's warmth and light are dazzled over a larger area of ground.

FOOD FOR WARMTH

Becoming wise to winter's magic is restorative, especially if you skip into the cold with an array of warming recipes, each peppered with ingredients to invigorate you. Delicious morning staples, such as oats and bananas, are thermogenic, which means they boost your internal temperature, helping the body produce heat with their slow energy release. Seasoned with an armament of protective and stimulating spices, your senses will be roused by the invitation of a new day.

RISE AND SHINE TISANE

After a long slumber, you emerge a little dehydrated. Drinking a large glass of water upon waking is one of the best ways to begin your day. This sunrise sip can restore hydration as well as improve gut health and boost energy.

To ensure I have a constant supply of lemons, I simply freeze halved lemons in an airtight container. You can use them straight from frozen, or defrost them in the refrigerator overnight. Evergreen bay is easy to access and I love to gather a fresh bouquet when I'm out on frosty strolls. In autumn, when fennel seeds are in abundance, I try to squirrel enough away to see me through the winter.

FOR EACH PERSON

½ lemon
½ tsp fennel seeds
1–2 bay leaves, fresh or dried (optional)
250ml freshly boiled water

Cut the lemon half into slices or wedges. Place in a teacup or teapot with the fennel seeds and bay leaves, if using, and pour over the boiling water.

Steep for 5–10 minutes, then strain, if you like, and drink.

FINNISH EMERGENCY BREAD

In Finland, *hätäleipä* means 'emergency bread'. Normally, it's a classic treacly, dark and dense sourdough rye. I've used kefir to aid in this bread emergency, which means you can make a sourdough loaf in twenty-four hours even if you don't have a starter on the go. The magic's in the curd-like culture used to make kefir, which contains up to twenty-eight different strains of gut-friendly bacteria who love a flour feast. When you hydrate a few shakes of rye with kefir, it creates more bubbles than a glass of champagne in just a few hours. Basically, the bacteria are belching with delight as they break down all the complex sugars in the flour, producing carbon dioxide which helps the bread rise as well as making it more digestible.

**MAKES 1 LOAF
(ABOUT 12 SERVINGS)**

For the overnight starter
75g rye flour, plus more if needed
150g unflavoured kefir (dairy kefir or water kefir), plus more if needed
50–100ml water, plus more if needed

For the loaf
200g overnight starter (see above)
150g kefir
185ml lukewarm water, plus more if needed
3 tbsp molasses
1 tsp coriander seeds
1 tsp caraway seeds
1 tbsp raw cacao powder (optional)
500g rye flour, plus more to dust
½ tsp sea salt
oil, for the dish or tray

Mix the flour and kefir until you have a smooth paste. Stir in enough water to create a double-cream consistency. This is your quick overnight starter. Cover with a plate or clean cloth and leave to ferment overnight, or until light and bubbly (about 12 hours). If it's slow to become bubbly, add 2 tbsp flour and a little more kefir (and water, if needed). This will give it an extra boost, which should do the trick. It should develop a sweet, almost apple-like smell. If you already have a rye starter on the go, just give it a feed with 75g rye flour and 150ml water and let it ferment overnight. Now you have the base for your loaf.

If you want to keep a rye starter on the go, spoon 2 tbsp of the bubbling starter into a jam jar to store in the refrigerator. It'll keep happily for 2 weeks without needing a feed, or you can freeze it. Having it to hand saves you making a starter when you make the loaf again.

Once you have a bubbling starter, spoon 200g of it into a large bowl. Add the 150g kefir, the lukewarm water (weighed on a scale for accuracy) and spoon in the molasses. Stir until well mixed, then stir in the spices and cacao, if using, followed by the flour and salt.

Mix thoroughly for 3 minutes. The dough will be soft and sticky, unlike conventional dough. It won't be stretchy, so you need a stirring action – rather than kneading – to bring it together.

Shape into a large, round loaf and place on a lightly oiled baking tray, or nestle into a large, lightly oiled, casserole dish, which will help it hold its shape. Scoop the dough into the oiled dish or on to a lightly oiled baking tray. Dust a little flour over the top and cover with a lightly dampened clean cloth. Set aside to rise for 8 hours (quite a long time, but it will depend on the strength of the starter and the ambient temperature). The dough is ready to cook when it has increased in size and has cracks from swelling (as in the photo on page 21).

Preheat the oven to 220°C/210°C fan. Set a baking tray full of water in the bottom of the oven, to create steam to help to loaf to rise further. Place the loaf in the centre of the oven and bake for 15 minutes.

Reduce the oven temperature to 180°C/170°C fan and bake for a further 45 minutes or until the bread has darkened, slightly cracked on top and sounds hollow when tapped.

Let the bread cool for 20 minutes before cutting into it. To retain freshness, wrap the loaf in a cloth and store at room temperature for up to 3 days, or slice and freeze it for instant rye sourdough toast opportunities: just pop a slice in the toaster and cook a touch longer from frozen. Works a treat.

Sourdough survival in the -30°C depths of Canada

Yukon is the smallest and most westerly of Canada's three territories. It is also the second-least populated province in Canada. In the depths of winter, the temperature (in degrees Celsius) nearly always has a minus sign in front of it. In February, -30°C is not uncommon. I honestly can't even fathom the impact and extent of such breathtaking subzero temperatures. Newcomers to the region are closely monitored (and supported) in winter. They even have a festival in February to keep morale high, as they all bolster themselves together against the last few months of intense coldness. Once you've survived your first winter in Yukon, locals call you a 'sourdough'. I love this. The nickname references the achievement of locals who manage to keep their sourdough starters alive despite the frosty thermostat. Sourdough thrives at around 22°C, so -30°C is a bit of a challenging temperature for the culture of bacteria and yeast. Some people nestle their starters in pockets next to their skin, using body heat to keep the culture warm enough to thrive and survive in the harsh winter.

There is a rich sourdough bread culture in the region, which migrated up from San Francisco – one of the most famous places for sourdough in the west – more than a century ago.

Ione Christensen deserves a medal for her sourdough survival skills. Astonishingly, her starter is more than 120 years old. It's been in her family since the 1898 Klondike Gold Rush, when her great-grandfather travelled to Dawson City via the Chilkoot Trail. Many Klondike stampeders relied on their ball of sourdough starter as they made the long journey to Dawson City. Christensen's prized starter was recently shipped to Saint-Vith, Belgium, to become sample 106 in the Puratos sourdough library, where bacterial analysis proved its century-plus survival. Christensen still uses her starter each weekend to make fluffy and flavourful sourdough waffles and hot cakes.

The sourdough tradition in Yukon is a beautiful illustration of how food sustains us in the harshest of times and climes.

TAHINI PEAR PORRIDGE

When my son was small, winter stirred us into porridge mode in the mornings. Chopped apple or pear with a pinch of spice have long been staple additions for us, but this is a new favourite. Tahini folded in at the end of cooking creates a richer, creamier body to the porridge and raises its calcium and B-vitamin content.

FOR EACH PERSON

1 pear
50g, or 4 tbsp, rolled oats
250–300ml milk of your choice, plus more to serve
good pinch of ground cardamom seeds and/or Masala chai
    (see page 231), or ground cinnamon, plus more to serve
small piece of finely grated root ginger (optional)
pinch of sea salt (optional)
1 tbsp tahini
drizzle of maple syrup, or honey, or a swirl of Spiced figgy jam
    (see page 44)

Core and finely chop half the pear, keeping the skin on. Put the chopped pear, all the oats and 250ml of the milk in a saucepan with a good pinch of your favourite spice. I love a generous pinch of ground cardamom or Masala chai (see page 231), as well as the warmth of cinnamon and freshly grated ginger. A pinch of salt adds a delicious contrast. Give everything a good stir in the pan before setting it over a medium heat.

For the creamiest consistency, stir constantly, as if you were making risotto, until all the milk is absorbed and the oats are tender, adding the remaining 50ml milk if needed.

Fold in the tahini and a splash more milk as soon as the porridge is done as you like it. Spoon into a bowl and top with the remaining pear half, finely sliced, a drizzle of maple syrup, honey or jam and a final dusting of spice.

BANANA BREAD BLINIS

This is a comforting marriage of two of my favourite things: banana bread and little buckwheat pancakes. After lots of experimenting, I distilled my idea of this union into a really simple, protein-packed recipe in which the fruit and nuts play a dominant role, both enhancing nutritional value and flavour. Delicious with a Steamy dandelion oat latte (see page 296).

MAKES ABOUT 24 BITE-SIZED
BLINIS, OR 12 LARGER PANCAKES

1 ripe banana
75g walnuts, or pecans
1 egg, or 1 tbsp ground flaxseed mixed with 2 tbsp water
75ml water
1 tbsp apple cider vinegar, or lemon juice
1 tbsp maple syrup, or honey, plus more (optional) to serve
2 tbsp buckwheat flour
2 tsp baking powder
2 tsp ground cinnamon, or mixed spice
pinch of sea salt
2 tbsp coconut oil, or ghee (for homemade, see page 214)

To serve (optional)
Roasted banana slices (see overleaf)
Maple walnuts or pecans (see overleaf)
maple syrup, or Banana skin honey (see overleaf)
kefir, or natural yogurt

Blend the banana and nuts until you have a smooth paste. Add the remaining ingredients apart from the oil or ghee and blend until smooth.

Set a large frying pan over a medium heat. Add 1 tsp of the coconut oil or ghee and swirl to melt, then whisk this into the batter.

Add a fresh gloss of oil or ghee to the pan, just enough to coat it. Dollop 1 tbsp batter into the pan for each blini, depending on how big you want them. You should be able to cook 2–3 blinis at a time. Cook for 2–3 minutes until the top of the pancakes starts to look set and lots of bubbles have formed.

Flip the pancakes over with a spatula or palette knife. Cook for another 2–3 minutes until golden brown and set underneath. Pop on a plate. Repeat until the batter is used up, adding more oil or ghee to the pan as you need it. You can keep the pancakes warm in a low oven as you cook them.

Delicious served with Roasted banana slices and Maple walnuts or pecans, but equally lovely with a simple drizzle of maple syrup or Banana skin honey and a dollop of kefir or yogurt.

ROASTED BANANA SLICES

Bananas have so much natural sugar that you needn't add anything further to sweeten them. The roasting here teases those sugars out, caramelising them into delicious chewy morsels to boost the banana in the blinis.

SERVES 4

1 tsp ghee (for homemade, see page 214), or coconut oil
2 bananas (½ banana for each person)

Preheat the oven to 180°C/170°C fan. Use the ghee or oil to lightly oil a baking tray. Cut the bananas into 1cm slices and arrange on the prepared tray. Roast for 15–20 minutes or until the slices are sticky and golden.

BANANA SKIN HONEY
Y

Banana skins are rich with nutrients and you can transform them into a stunning honey by finely slicing and bundling them into a jar with enough honey to fully coat and cover. It'll ferment (a good thing) as it infuses over 1–2 weeks, intensifying in flavour. Strain off the skins and use the honey to drizzle over Banana bread blinis or Banana split (see pages 26 and 254), or whip into a thick, creamy banana-honey butter.

MAPLE WALNUTS OR PECANS

A simple crunchy topping to add a little sweetness and protein to Banana bread blinis, Tahini pear porridge or the Boosted Bircher bowl (see pages 26, 24 and 50).

SERVES 4

100g walnuts, or pecans
2 tbsp maple syrup
pinch of sea salt (oak-smoked salt is lovely here)

Preheat the oven to 180°C/170°C fan. Mix the nuts, maple syrup and salt in a roasting dish. Roast for 15–20 minutes or until caramelised.

SOAKED CHIA SEEDS

Ancient Aztec and Mayan civilisations knew the medicinal worth of chia seeds. Not only are they the richest plant source of omega-3 fatty acids, they are a good source of calcium and a complete protein, containing all nine essential amino acids that cannot be made by the body. Eating them in the morning offers further benefits, giving your digestive system a boost. I tend to soak a few tablespoons at a time so I can use them on a whim, adding to smoothies, porridge, granola, kefir and soups to boost nutrient value and create a thicker, more satisfying consistency. You can use soaked (aka 'activated') chia seeds in place of dried in any of these recipes, remembering that 10g dried seeds = 20g soaked seeds.

ENOUGH FOR 2–4 SERVINGS

4 tbsp chia seeds
250ml water

Tip the chia seeds into a jam jar. Stir in the water. Seal the lid and chill for 15 minutes or until the seeds absorb the water, creating a seedy jelly. Store in the refrigerator for up to 1 week.

GOLDEN SPICED CHIA

Y

Use coconut milk in place of the water and add a thumb of finely grated root turmeric or 1 tsp ground turmeric, a twist of freshly ground black pepper and 1 tsp Masala chai (see page 231), or ground cinnamon.

Wheatgrass

A shot of freshly juiced wheatgrass in the morning is especially beneficial in the winter, as its chlorophyll can detoxify the body, aid in weight management and stimulate blood circulation, which in turn will help keep you warm and improve digestion, resulting in higher energy levels. Wheatgrass is known to increase red blood cell count, which enhances the immunity of the body and helps to keep common diseases such as flu, coughs and colds and other infections at bay.

You can buy trays of living wheatgrass to feed through a juicer, but if you're lacking in time, space or a juicer, frozen wheatgrass juice and powdered wheatgrass are the next best things.

Wheatgrass is easy to grow; it takes ten days from seed. These instructions will give you about a week's worth of harvests. For continuous wheatgrass harvesting and drinking, it's worth having two or three trays on the go, sowing one every seven to ten days.

YOU WILL NEED

1 heavy-duty seed tray (bamboo trays are great), recommended dimensions 37 × 21.5cm
1 litre organic compost
500g organic wheat or spelt grain

GROWING AND HARVESTING

Fill the tray with compost, pat it down, then pour over enough water to really moisten (not drench) the soil.

Scatter a thick, single-layered carpet of seeds over the top. Pat these down.

Cover the seeds with a 1–2cm layer of compost. Smooth over, patting down to nestle everything into the tray.

Cover the tray with a damp cloth and keep in a dark, warm place, such as on top of the refrigerator, or near a radiator.

Mist the cloth covering the seed tray once or twice a day.

After five to seven days, the seeds should be swollen and starting to push the cloth up. Remove the cloth and move the seeds to a windowsill, or somewhere with direct sunlight.

Continue watering, keeping the growing grass and compost moist.

Start harvesting when your wheatgrass is about 10cm tall. Continue harvesting until the wheatgrass stops growing.

For a shot for one person (about 40ml), juice 50g (a generous fistful) of freshly harvested wheatgrass.

CARROT CAKE FLAPJACKS

These have the most heavenly carrot cake-like flavour and texture, making them wildly indulgent as well as deliciously nourishing. Their sweetness comes from dates, which are full of fibre, as well as honey, which you can omit to reduce the content of sugars, if needed.

I love having these with a cup of Apple scraps chai (see page 272).

MAKES 12–16

150g walnuts, or any nuts or seeds
2 carrots (total weight 200g)
200g jumbo porridge oats
1 clementine
125g coconut oil
125g pitted dates
2 tbsp raw honey (optional)
3cm thumb of root ginger, finely grated
1 tbsp mixed spice
¼ tsp ground cloves
¼ tsp ground cardamom
50g ground flaxseed, and/or hemp seeds

Preheat the oven to 180°C/170°C fan.

Line a 20cm square tin with greaseproof paper – this will stop the flapjacks sticking to the tin – or use a tin with a removable base.

Roughly chop the nuts. Coarsely grate the carrots. Mix both together with the oats in a large bowl.

In a blender, whizz the whole clementine – skin and all – with the coconut oil, dates, honey, if using, ginger, spices and flaxseed or hemp seeds. Pour the spiced date mixture in with the nuts, carrots and oats and mix.

Pack into the lined tin, pressing down to compact the mix, and bake in the centre of the oven for 30 minutes, or until golden on the top and crispy around the edges. Cut the flapjack into 12–16 rectangular or square bars and store in the refrigerator for up to 1 week.

MISO MUSHROOM PORRIDGE

Mushrooms are like sun sponges. They contain a compound called ergosterol which, when exposed to sunlight, transforms into vitamin D. Any mushrooms can be exposed to sunlight at any point to enrich their vitamin D content, even dried mushrooms from the supermarket that have been grown indoors under artificial light. Put the mushrooms in sunlight for six to eight hours at any point up to a month before consuming them and they will experience the heightened levels of vitamin D. That's definitely a reason to incorporate more mushrooms into your diet in the winter, when sunlight is scarce and vitamin D levels are low. Using dried mushrooms in this recipe also means you get your porridge fix faster.

FOR EACH PERSON

10g dried mushrooms (I love shiitake here)
250ml freshly boiled water, or coffee (regular or dandelion coffee, see page 296, or a mix)
50g rolled buckwheat groats, raw or toasted
1 tbsp finely grated root ginger
2 tsp miso (any kind is fine)
splash of tamari, soy sauce, or 1 tsp Black garlic teriyaki (see page 210)
good grinding of black pepper

To serve (optional)
1 egg yolk
dusting of Mushroom furikake (see page 224)

Soak the dried mushrooms in a small bowl in 100ml of the boiling water, or freshly brewed coffee, for 15 minutes, or until plump and tender (they will cook further in the porridge).

Put the mushrooms and buckwheat groats in a saucepan with their soaking liquid and the remaining measured water or coffee, the ginger and a good twist of pepper. Give everything a good stir in the pan, then set it over a medium heat. Once warm and steamy, stir in the miso.

For the creamiest consistency, stir constantly, as if you were making risotto, until all the water is absorbed and the buckwheat groats are tender, adding more water, if needed. It'll take about 20 minutes over a medium-low heat for the buckwheat to absorb most of the liquid and become tender.

Once the groats are tender, season the porridge with tamari, soy sauce or Black garlic teriyaki and more black pepper to taste.

Spoon into a bowl. This is delicious as is but, for a sunny, protein-rich finish, you can cradle a raw egg yolk (it will cook a little in the residual heat) into the centre of the porridge and finish with a dusting of furikake.

SOLAR-POWERED YOLKS

Hens slow down, or even stop, egg production during the autumn and winter, due to the shorter hours of light and colder weather. These changes signal to their bodies to rest – to conserve energy and stay warm – rather than continue to lay eggs.

PARISIAN OMELETTE CRÊPES

When egg production is low (see page 35), this recipe is perfect, as an omelette crêpe only requires a single egg. If it's an outdoor-reared organic egg, it will be solar-charged with immune-boosting vitamin D.

FOR EACH CRÊPE

1 egg
1 small garlic clove
½ tsp Dijon mustard
2 tsp chopped herb leaves (thyme, parsley, oregano)
1 tsp ghee (for homemade, see page 214), butter, or oil
sea salt and freshly ground black pepper

To serve (optional)
kimchi (for homemade, see page 206)
hot sauce
L'escargot mushrooms (see page 86)

Set a large frying pan over a high heat. Crack an egg into a bowl. Peel and finely grate in the garlic, then whisk in the Dijon mustard and half the herbs and season the mixture.

Brush the hot pan with the ghee, butter or oil.

Add the whisked egg mixture. Swirl the pan around to distribute the egg in the pan, as if you were making a crêpe.

Cook until golden on the bottom and just about set on the top (no need to flip). Fold over once or twice. Each omelette crêpe only takes a minute or 2 to make.

Pop on to a plate. (Keep warm in a low oven if making more than one.)

Finish with the remaining herbs, as well as kimchi, hot sauce or your favourite topping, if you like. I love these with L'escargot mushrooms.

WOODSTOCK FRYING PAN GRANOLA

I have a weak spot for crunchy clusters of sweetened oats packed with nuts, seeds and dried fruit. Admittedly, this is what I have for dinner when I'm working late and don't feel like cooking, while my teenage son relies on it as a pre-breakfast snack. It's a great thing to crave when you have the munchies, especially homemade versions, which are lighter on sugar.

Granola (originally spelled 'granula') was created by Dr James Caleb Jackson for his health spa in Dansville, New York, in 1863. Just over a century later, a version – featuring soy sauce as a salty foil to honey – famously fed 400,000 hungry revellers at Woodstock as a large-scale 'breakfast in bed' on Max Yasgur's dairy farm.

You could easily make this granola at a festival any time of the year, and you can amp the numbers up by 100,000. But this recipe is a small-batch affair, made in minutes using just a frying pan to lap up the heat as you give the mixture the few stirs it needs before it's ready to eat.

Buckwheat and quinoa are both rich in protein and both are seeds rather than grains, but if you want a more paleo or keto option, you can swap them or the oats for more seeds and nuts, and swap the sweetener for more oil, which will help bind everything together. Adding more spices will further boost the natural sweetness of the remaining ingredients.

MAKES 300G, OR 4 SERVINGS

100g cashews, or any seeds or nuts
50g desiccated coconut, or chia seeds (soaked if you like, see page 30)
150g porridge oats, or buckwheat groats, or sprouted quinoa (see page 66)
pinch of ground cinnamon and/or ground cardamom seeds
2 tbsp maple syrup, puréed dates, or Spiced figgy jam (see page 44)
1 tbsp coconut oil, or olive oil, or Golden butter (see page 212) for
   a gilded granola
shake of soy sauce, or a hint of miso (optional)
1 tbsp any booster powder (optional, see page 48)

Set a large frying pan over a medium heat. Mix all the ingredients apart from the booster powder, if using, in a large bowl. Scrunch together to mix well and create granola-like clusters.

Scatter the ingredients across the frying pan in an even layer. Gently cook for 10 minutes, stirring often, or until the nuts start to toast a little. Leave to cool, then add the booster powder, if using (so you don't damage its benefits).

The granola will be soft until it's fully cooled, then it'll turn nice and crunchy. But if you want to eat sooner, spoon it into a bowl and – as soon as cold milk hits it – the granola will crisp up.

OVERNIGHT FIVE SEED BREAD

When the temperature drops outside, our energy levels and metabolism tend to take a dip as well. There's a bounty of foods that can give you a boost and seeds come high on the list. This loaf abounds with sunflower, pumpkin, chia and flaxseed or hemp seeds, all of which are rich sources of the fatty acids and fibre that are known to fuel energy. To top up the seedy goodness, you can add 1 tsp each of fennel and coriander seeds.

To bind all the protein-packed seeds together, I've simply added oats, a rich source of both soluble and insoluble fibre. The soluble fibre absorbs water and becomes a viscous gel as it moves through the gastrointestinal tract, soothing the tract, as well as feeding the good bacteria in your gut. The insoluble fibre acts like a broom to sweep the colon free of toxins.

**MAKES 1 LARGE LOAF
OR 2 SMALLER LOAVES**

150g sunflower seeds
150g pumpkin seeds
1 tsp apple cider vinegar
50g chia seeds (soaked, if you like, see page 30)
100g rolled oats
25g ground flaxseed, or hemp seeds
½ tsp sea salt
75g tahini, or any nut or seed butter
2 tbsp maple syrup, or molasses
150ml water

Soak the sunflower and pumpkin seeds in a bowl in enough water to fully cover, adding the vinegar, for 4 hours or overnight. Drain and rinse.

Preheat the oven to 180°C/170°C fan. Line a loaf tin with greaseproof paper; this dough will make enough for 1 × 900g loaf tin, or 2 × 450g tins.

Mix the drained seeds and remaining ingredients until you have a smooth doughy paste. Let it sit for 20 minutes, so the oats and flax can absorb the water. Spoon the dough into the tin(s), filling just to the top, and smooth over. If you have extra dough, try making Seedy crackers (see opposite).

Bake in the centre of the oven for 1 hour. If you cook 2 × 450g loaves at once, the cooking time is pretty much the same as for 1 × 900g loaf. Whichever you're baking, ensure the bread is nicely golden, pulled away from the sides of the tin a bit and that a knife inserted into the centre comes out clean. Remove it from the oven and cool for 10–15 minutes, then remove from the tin. If the base and sides aren't nicely golden, flash back in the oven, upside down, for 15 minutes to brown them.

Let cool for 15 minutes before slicing.

SEEDY CRACKERS

Lightly oil 2 sheets of greaseproof paper. Use lightly oiled hands to bundle any leftover dough into your hands and start patting into a thin rectangle on a sheet of paper. Once you have a relatively thin layer with fairly neat sides, cover with the other sheet of paper and use a rolling pin to get it as thin as possible (aim for the thickness of a penny). Try to keep the dough as smooth and even as you can. Transfer to a baking tray and bake in an oven preheated to 180°C/170°C fan, initially sandwiched between both sheets of greaseproof paper, for 15 minutes, or until the crackers are firm. Remove the top sheet of paper and let the crackers crisp on top. I like to add a sprinkling of salt at this point, or spices such as chilli flakes and fennel seeds. Check the base of the crackers after the tops are golden, as you may want to flip them over to crisp on the underside. Cut into squares or break into shards. Delicious (and pictured on page 71) with Mushroom and black garlic paté.

APPLE ALMOND SCONES

Finely grating raw apples creates a juicy and fresh apple sauce that lends the perfect hint of sweetness and just the right amount of moisture to these super-simple soda bread-like scones. The ground almonds and buckwheat make them gluten-free and protein-rich. They're delicious for breakfast, but equally gorgeous alongside soup.

MAKES 6

oil or butter, for the tray
2 apples
1 tbsp ground flaxseed
2 tsp gluten-free baking powder
1 tbsp water, plus more if needed
75g buckwheat flour, plus more if needed
50g ground almonds
pinch of sea salt (oak-smoked salt is lovely here)

Preheat the oven to 180°C/170°C fan. Lightly coat a baking tray with oil or butter.

Finely grate the apples, skin and all, discarding or composting the stems and cores. You want 200g, but if its slightly over or under you can make a note of the weight and compensate by adding more or less flour in the next step.

Fold the ground flaxseed and baking powder into the apple along with the measured water. Fold in the buckwheat flour, ground almonds and a pinch of salt.

Gently combine until it comes together into a soft, workable dough: add more flour if it's too wet, or a little water if it's too dry. Shape into a rectangle 2–3cm thick, then cut into 6 equal-sized squares or wedges and place on the prepared baking sheet.

Bake in the oven for 15–18 minutes until risen, golden and the bases sound hollow when tapped. Allow to cool for 5 minutes before eating.

SPICED FIGGY JAM

Dried figs are used in herbal medicine for treating ailments including colds, flu and winter coughs. Which makes this either a brilliant winter-morning fruity spread for toast, a compote to dollop on porridge, or an added boost to a Bircher bowl. It's particularly delicious paired with tahini.

The addition of citrus juice offers a healthy dose of vitamin C, which helps your body to absorb the iron in the figs.

For a variation, swap the orange juice for pomegranate and add 1–2 tsp rose water.

MAKES 200G

100g dried figs (5–6)
150ml freshly squeezed blood orange juice, or any orange juice, or clementine juice
½ tsp Masala chai (see page 231)

Place the figs in a saucepan with the juice (grate in some zest before juicing your citrus, if you like).

Gently simmer the figs in the juice for 10 minutes, or until they're soft enough to blend into a purée.

Blend the figs with the juice and spice until smooth. Store in a jam jar in the refrigerator for up to 1 month.

DRIED ORANGE ZEST

Any time you are using citrus, consider paring off the zest with a veg peeler and drying the strips. To dry, simply arrange the strips on a clean cloth or wooden board (this helps absorb moisture). Leave to dry for 3–4 days, then store in a lidded jar for up to 1 year. The dried zest can be added to all manner of dishes, such as Rayu, or try it in a festive pan of Mulled hibiscus or Christmas tree tea (see pages 194, 284 and 276).

Winter spa smoothies

Leafy greens, such as spinach or kale, are excellent sources of fibre, as well as nutrients such as folate, vitamin C, vitamin K and vitamin A. Research shows that they also contain a specific type of sugar that helps fuel the growth of healthy gut bacteria.

Eating a lot of fibre and leafy greens allows you to develop an ideal gut microbiome: those trillions of organisms that live in the colon. A healthy gut translates to better nutrient intake, which improves energy levels and overall physical and mental health.

My friend and former colleague Nadia Brydon is a naturopath and, during her training as a practitioner in public health, documented the benefits of adding a green smoothie to your day. Even if you change nothing else, her studies proved that simply adding the smoothie had a positive impact on blood sugar levels in diabetics.

The advantage smoothies have over juices is that they contain all the fibre of their raw ingredients, which gives them the gut-friendly edge. I've created a canvas here to inspire you to make something wonderfully crave-worthy, both for its delicious taste and its positive effects.

FOR EACH PERSON

ANATOMY OF THE PERFECT GREEN SMOOTHIE

BODY 1 pear, 1 apple, ½ avocado, 1 banana or 1 ripe persimmon.

GREENS a large handful (50–75g) of spinach, kale, watercress, wild greens such as dandelions, nettles and cleavers, or in the absence of fresh greens use 1 tbsp spirulina, chlorella or wheatgrass powder (see pages 49 and 302).

HEALTHY FATS 1–2 tbsp soaked and drained nuts or seeds, nut or seed butter, linseed oil or other omega-rich and nutritionally-dense cold-pressed oils such as blackcurrant seed or pumpkin seed. I use more of these if I'm blending a smoothie with water rather than a nut milk, which I think is a purer approach. I also use more fat if I'm having my smoothie as a meal.

A VITAMIN C BOOST TO HELP YOU ABSORB MORE IRON FROM THE GREENS 1 tbsp fresh citrus juice, plus a good ½–1 tsp grating of zest, or in the absence of citrus use apple cider vinegar.

BOOSTER POWDER (SEE PAGE 48) these are optional, but using a nutritionally dense powder means you can target different needs, such as hormones, energy or immunity. Read the dosage instructions on the packet, but I normally add 1 tbsp in total. My favourites include energising *maca*, immune-boosting *chaga*, *brahmi* for brain health and *shatavari* to help balance hormones.

SPICE this adds culinary flair, natural sweetness and a medicinal boost. Try ¼–½ tsp ground cardamom seeds, cinnamon or Masala chai (see page 231).

LIQUID about 400ml filtered water or plant-based milk to bring it all together. It's best to avoid dairy for green smoothies, as the calcium in dairy can inhibit the body from absorbing the iron in the greens.

Y Blend all the ingredients together, adding more water, if needed. Whizz in a pitted date, other dried fruit or a little honey, if it needs a bit of added sweetness.

Y Pour into a glass and drink straight away.

Booster powders

I love to have a pantry full of different booster powders to add a vitamin boost to smoothies (see previous page), porridge and Bircher bowls. There are many more booster powders beyond the list that follows, but these are those that I use and love. They're great at targeting winter illness: they boost immunity, give you energy and make you feel happy. Do take care with them, however, as they can be very potent. Cross-check the suggested serving size (normally from 1 tsp to 1 tbsp) on the packet and make sure it won't interfere with any medications you might be taking. If you're new to using booster powders, it's wise to start with a smaller quantity and increase it gradually over time. Also, I find variety the best approach: rather than focusing on one booster, I try to mix it up every few days, trying three to five different boosters in a week.

IMMUNE BOOSTING

CAMU CAMU   An evergreen shrub that grows in swampy or flooded areas of the Amazon rainforest. Its small fruit is very acidic and sour and is believed to have the highest naturally occurring vitamin C content of any plant in the world.

GINSENG   Siberian ginseng was traditionally used to prevent colds and flu and to increase energy, longevity and vitality. It is widely used in Russia to help the body better cope with either mental or physical stress. It has a slightly bitter flavour, married with parsnip tones, but is relatively mild and starchy because, as with parsnip, it's the root that's harvested.

MORINGA   This powder is harvested from the green leaves of a large tree native to Africa. The leaves have seven times more vitamin C than oranges and fifteen times more potassium than bananas. Many people add it to smoothies as a daily multivitamin. It has high antibiotic and antibacterial properties which can help combat infections. Flavour-wise, it's like a stronger, powdered form of spinach.

REISHI   A reddish-brown kidney-shaped fungus native to Asia, with bands that lend it a distinctly fan-like appearance. The mushroom is said to improve the function of adrenal glands by working on the hypothalamus-pituitary-adrenal gland axis. This makes *reishi* an excellent herb choice for calming the mind, easing anxiety and promoting sleep. Beyond an obvious mushroomy note, *reishi* has hits of chocolate, veering towards the more bitter side.

SEA BUCKTHORN   The world's richest source of omega-7, which helps to promote healthier hair, skin and nails. It's also rich in vitamins A and C, both of which help support immune function. The finely milled sea buckthorn berry seeds have a tangy taste with a citrus zing. It's a brilliant replacement for citrus in recipes.

ENERGISING

MACA   Known as Peruvian ginseng, *maca* has been heralded for centuries in the Andes for its energy-yielding properties, which are down to its rich iron content. This also benefits the immune system. *Maca* is used to help calm hormonal imbalances in women caused by the menopause. It has a caramel-like flavour, making it a delicious natural sweetener.

SPIRULINA   A blue-green algae, believed to be one of the oldest life forms on Earth. The Aztecs used it as an endurance-booster to fuel marathons and more, due to its high protein levels. Adding it to a green smoothie can offer an instant energy boost. The flavour might not be to everyone's taste. I call it 'pond scum', as it has a really fishy-meets-seaweed taste (not so good in porridge!) but I've come to love it, even crave it in a green smoothie, due its energy-boosting results.

BRAIN FUELLING

ASHWAGANDHA   Harvested roots from the African winter cherry evergreen shrub. The root contains chemicals that might help calm the brain, reduce swelling and blood pressure and boost the immune system. In Ayurvedic medicine, it's used to combat stress and anxiety, as well as to ease insomnia. Flavour-wise, it's quite earthy and a little bitter, like raw cacao mixed with dandelion.

BRAHMI   The light, cocoa-like powder made from this green herb – also known as water hyssop, thyme-leaved gratiola and herb of grace – is a staple in traditional Ayurvedic medicine and most highly praised for its brain-boosting benefits. Studies show regular consumption can have a positive impact on memory, attention and the ability to process information. It has bitter walnut-like notes, with hints of dried porcini.

CHLORELLA   A blue-green algae native to Japan, *chlorella* is full of antioxidants such as omega-3s, vitamin C and carotenoids like beta-carotene and lutein. These nutrients fight cell damage in our bodies and help reduce the risk of diabetes, cognitive disease, heart problems and cancer. It has a rich, seaweedy flavour, a touch milder than spirulina and more like watercress.

SHATAVARI   This ancient root is great for woman at any age from puberty to menopause. Promoting sexual health, it also balances the hormonal system by regulating oestrogen production. If you battle cramps or irregular hormones, this herb can be a game changer. But it's not just for women: the asparagus-related root can help reduce stress, calm the mind and increase blood circulation in men (in all areas). The taste of *shatavari* is mild, it's a light powder with a hint of bitterness married with vanilla.

BOOSTED BIRCHER BOWL

My bircher is inspired by the Swiss physician Maximilian Oskar Bircher-Benner, who's famous for popularising muesli. After studying medicine at the University of Zurich, he opened his own clinic... but shortly after, developed jaundice and cured himself – according to legend – by eating raw apples! He expanded his nutritional research and opened a sanatorium called Vital Force in 1897. Bircher-Benner believed raw fruits and vegetables held the most nutritional value and his muesli was focused around raw oats mixed with raw fruit and nuts or seeds.

This is one of my staples and it's the perfect fast-breaker to fuel me through a winter day. I swap between this and a green smoothie as a weekday, work-from-home brunch. As with the Winter spa smoothies (see page 46), this recipe is meant more as a blueprint than a strict and structured formula, to inspire variety and also to let you create with confidence, using the ingredients you love and have to hand.

FOR EACH PERSON

200g kefir, or natural yogurt, or plant-based alternative
1 grated apple, pear, or carrot (I love purple carrot here)
2 tbsp oats
1 tbsp nuts and/or seeds
1 tsp booster powder, such as *maca* and *brahmi* (see page 49)
1 tsp flaxseed oil, or a cold-pressed omega-rich oil such as blackcurrant seed or pumpkin seed and/or 1 tsp nut or seed butter such as tahini
1 tsp Spiced figgy jam (see page 44), honey, or dried fruit (optional)

Use your bowl as a canvas and start adding the paint in the form of kefir and grated fruit or veg.

Scatter with oats, nuts and/or seeds, a dusting of a booster powder and a drizzle of oil or dollop of nut or seed butter.

Finish with a hint of sweetness, if you like, and tuck in.

KIMCHI BOKKEUMBAP

Kimchi fried rice is the ultimate Korean comfort food. Best of all, if you have cold cooked rice in the refrigerator, it takes only minutes to make and is not only healthier for your gut (see page 154), but also has a better texture for frying.

FOR EACH PERSON

150–200g cold, cooked brown basmati rice, or short grain rice
   (see How to cook perfect rice, page 223)
1 tsp sesame oil
100g kimchi
1 tbsp ghee (for homemade, see page 214), or coconut oil

To serve (optional)
fried egg
handful of finely chopped spring onions, three-cornered leek and/or sesame
   seeds, or Mushroom furikake (see page 224)

Use day-old rice. This allows the starch in the rice to retrograde, which makes it much easier to flake apart, but more importantly, it's better for your gut health (see page 154 for more on this). Drizzle the sesame oil over the rice: this infuses it with flavour as well as separates the individual grains so you can stir-fry them more effectively.

Set a sieve over a bowl. Place the kimchi in the sieve and press out all the delicious juices that are teeming with good bacteria (you'll add them at the end to keep their live bacteria intact). You still get benefit from cooking the veg themselves, as the fermentation process makes them easier to digest while also boosting their vitamin C.

Set a large frying pan or wok over a medium-high heat. Add half the ghee or coconut oil and the rice. Arrange the rice in a single layer and let it sizzle undisturbed for a minute or so, or until it starts to brown a little on the bottom.

Fold the rice in the pan so you have the uncaramelised rice grains now on the base. Add the drained and squeezed kimchi to the rice along with the remaining ghee or oil and stir-fry, just for a few minutes, over a fairly high heat, until the rice has a nice colour and it's all warmed through.

Spoon on to a plate, or into a bowl and add the reserved kimchi brine to season.

Cap the rice with a fried egg and/or a handful of chopped spring onions or three-cornered leek (the foraged precursor to wild garlic) and/or a dusting of sesame seeds or furikake.

SNACKS,

SALADS

AND
SIDES

Winter is the sleeping space,
triggering a craving for slowness.
It's wise to indulge.

The instinct to rest in the still season – between the falling of the last leaves and the emergence of the first bud from the wakening soil – resonates with our ancient rhythms. We should listen, and revel in the soft sounds of quiet. Clarity is its gift.

WINTER VEG IS SWEETER

The best winter recipes sing of such simplicity and celebrate the unadulterated pleasures of nature's edible offerings. Raw carrots kissed with lemon, garlic and thyme: the perfect cold remedy, and delicious, too. The sweetness of caramelised parsnips warmed by a touch of ginger and the tang of citrus. Mushrooms roasted with nothing other than a pinch of salt to tease out their moisture while intensifying their meaty depth, then enrobed in a classic parsley and garlic butter.

When temperatures drop below freezing, frost triggers certain plants to produce more sugar. Root vegetables including carrots, beetroot, turnips, swede and parsnips, as well as brassicas such as cabbages, Brussels sprouts, cauliflower and kale, have the ability to convert some of their starch stores into sugar. They do this to keep the water in their cells from freezing. The adaptation keeps them from dying in the cold and, in the process, it makes them sweeter and more delicious.

It's far easier to take a pure approach to crafting winter kitchen wonders if you have well-sourced ingredients. A farmer's nurture is where the true art of cooking lies. The food of the colder months should sing out echoes of Romanian sculptor Constantin Brâncuşi's statement: 'simplicity is complexity resolved'.

Winter brings pleasures
of which summer knows nothing.

OYSTERS WITH HORSERADISH ICE

Oysters are the richest food source of zinc and just two of them can provide your total daily zinc needs. Our bodies can't produce zinc, so food and supplements are the most effective ways to boost your intake. Zinc's role in our bodies is to support the growth and functioning of immune cells: even a mild or moderate deficiency can slow down the activity of the lymphocytes, neutrophils and macrophages that protect against viruses and bacteria.

I like this fun twist of serving oysters with freshly grated frozen horseradish; it gives them a hint of nose-tingly heat, plus the benefits from the grated horseradish include sinus clearing, as well as further immune boosting.

If you've never shucked an oyster, give it a go. The first time I ever tried was on my birthday – during the Covid lockdowns – when my partner bought us a dozen oysters to have at home, to enjoy with local fizz. Learning to shuck oysters was a brilliant and unexpected birthday gift, and the results are deliciously rewarding!

SERVES 4

8–12 oysters
2–3cm piece of horseradish root, frozen
½ lemon, cut into wedges

Keep the oysters in the refrigerator until ready to serve and shuck them just before eating (see below).

Once shucked, finely grate a little dusting of frozen horseradish root over the top: literally, just a kiss of horseradish, as you don't want to overpower them. Serve with the lemon wedges.

OYSTER SHUCKING
Y

Put the whole oysters in a colander and rinse them with running water. Don't soak them in water though, or they'll become waterlogged.

The oysters have a distinct seam along the edge and there's a natural opening in this at the back of each oyster. With a tea towel protecting your hands, stick your shucker (oyster knife) into the little gap, press the knife in and then give it a little wiggly twist. Once in, gently run the shucker around the seam.

If the juice in the shell looks gritty, or has any shell in it, pour it through a sieve lined with muslin into a jug, then pour it back into the shells: the juice is wonderfully salty, a true delicious taste of the sea.

LIGURIAN LEEK PANCAKES

Around the world, there are many names for and variations on pancakes, breads and even a form of tofu made with chickpea flour. My favourite take is the Ligurian street food called *farinata*. I've been making these on my River Cottage fermentation courses for years and the best part about making them is having leftover batter in the freezer or refrigerator. Recently, I had a defrosted jar of batter in the refrigerator that needed using up. I also had a glut of leeks (and little else).

Hungry and in need of a quick-fix lunch, I made this and was sold. It's now my favourite way to use the batter. You could add any finely chopped or grated veg to the batter in place of leeks, but I think this is a great way to celebrate the elongated alliums, giving them a starring role, rather than that of a back-up singer. Leeks are great for you, too: they're probiotic, which means they're brilliant food for the bacteria in your gut, keeping them (and thus you) happy.

The fermentation process is an important step. Not only does it make the bean or pea flour more digestible, but it adds a phenomenal layer of flavour.

I love serving 2–3 of these as a light lunch with a dollop of Kefir labneh rippled through with a bit of Levantine garlic paste (see pages 256 and 216).

MAKES ABOUT 12

100g chickpea (gram) flour, or yellow pea flour
200–250ml kombucha, or whey from making Kefir labneh (see page 256), or a 50:50 mix of kefir or Greek yogurt with water
2 leeks
2–3 rosemary sprigs
2–3 tbsp coconut oil, or ghee (for homemade, see page 214)
sea salt and freshly ground black pepper

Whisk the flour and 200ml of the kombucha, whey or watered-down kefir or Greek yogurt in a bowl until you have a smooth batter the consistency of double cream. Add more liquid, if needed, until you achieve the correct consistency. Cover and leave to ferment at room temperature for at least 4 hours, or overnight. Refrigerate the bowl after 12 hours if you're not using it straight away (the batter base for the pancakes, with or without the added leeks, will happily keep in the refrigerator for 1 week, or you can freeze it, defrost in the refrigerator and use once defrosted).

Wash the leeks, thinly slice them and then it's worth giving them a further rinse, to ensure you eliminate any grit. Strip the leaves from the rosemary and finely chop them. Fold the chopped leek and rosemary through the fermented batter: you should have about an equal volume of leeks to batter (don't worry, it'll hold together). Season well.

Preheat the oven to 150°C/140°C fan, with a baking tray on the top shelf. Set a large frying pan over a high heat. Add enough oil or ghee to lightly coat. Spoon 1–2 large dessertspoons of the battered leeks into the hot oiled pan. Spread and smooth the mixture with the back of the spoon into a round, thin pancake. Cook for 2–3 minutes, or until set and golden on the base. Flip and cook until coloured on the other side.

Slide the cooked pancake on to the hot baking tray in the oven. Continue until you've used up all the batter or made as many pancakes as you want.

WILD AND SPROUTED FALAFEL WITH CARDAMOM-LIME TAHINI

Falafel is traditionally made with soaked dried chickpeas, but soaking the peas for a little longer than usual – until they start to sprout – makes them both easier to digest and more nutritious.

I love this recipe not only for its perfect illustration of how to embrace the joys of sprouting peas and beans, but also because of the warming Lebanese seven-spice blend. You can buy it in some shops and online, but I love making my own (do scale it up, if you like, and use 1 scant tablespoon in this recipe).

The wild food element is optional here – you can easily swap the wild greens with a handful of winter herbs or greens such as coriander leaves, spinach or kale – but trying to find some is a great excuse to venture outside to stretch your legs and fill your lungs with fresh air.

You can swap the lime in the tahini for any citrus, as long as you stick to the quantities of 1 tsp finely grated zest and 4 tbsp juice.

MAKES 10–12

For the Lebanese seven-spice
½ tsp ground cumin
½ tsp ground coriander
½ tsp freshly ground black pepper
¼ tsp ground cinnamon
⅛ tsp ground ginger, or 1 tsp freshly grated root ginger
⅛ tsp ground allspice
⅛ tsp ground nutmeg

For the falafel
200g sprouted chickpeas, or sprouted green peas, or fava beans/dried broad
    beans (see page 66)
15g seasonal or wild greens, such as three-cornered leek (or see
    recipe introduction)
½ leek, 2 spring onions, or 5g three-cornered leek, roughly chopped
1 tsp sumac, or 1 tbsp lemon juice
good pinch of sea salt
50g sesame seeds
2 tbsp coconut oil, or ghee (for homemade, see page 214)

For the cardamom-lime tahini
4 tbsp tahini
2 limes (or see recipe introduction)
2–4 tbsp water
1 small garlic clove
½ tsp ground cardamom seeds
sea salt

Mix all the ingredients for the seven-spice in a small bowl.

Place all the ingredients for the falafel apart from the sesame seeds and coconut oil or ghee in a food processor with the seven-spice (use 1 scant tbsp, if you scaled up the spice mixture).

Blend until everything comes together into a finely chopped dough-like mixture, then roll it into smooth walnut-sized balls.

Tip the sesame seeds into a large dish. Roll the falafels through the sesame seeds until nicely coated. Chill for at least 30 minutes, or up to 24 hours, in the refrigerator.

Meanwhile, preheat the oven to 200°C/190°C fan. Place a baking dish, big enough to hold all the falafel with space between them, in the oven to heat up.

Remove the preheated baking dish from the oven. Add the coconut oil or ghee and slip the dish back in the oven for a minute to help it fully melt. Remove and roll the sesame seed-coated falafel through the warm fat, coating all over.

Making sure there's plenty of space between the falafels, slide the dish into the oven and bake for 15–20 minutes or until golden and crisp on the outside.

While they are baking, measure the tahini into a bowl. Add the finely grated zest of 1 lime, 4 tbsp lime juice and 2 tbsp water to begin with, adding more water if needed to get a smooth, single-cream consistency. Grate in the garlic and add the cardamom and a pinch of salt, adjusting the seasoning to taste. Serve the warm falafel with the tahini.

The falafel freeze beautifully before or after cooking and you can reheat them from frozen, cooking at the same temperature as above, until warmed through. From frozen, pre-cooked falafel will need 35 minutes and raw falafel will need 45 minutes in the oven.

An indoor winter garden

Sprouting seeds, grains and pulses not only helps you transform something dormant from your kitchen cupboard into a nutrient-rich, living food, it's also an easy and cheap way to create delicious ingredients ripe for culinary experimentation. Sprouting is also the perfect growing project for winter. A further benefit is that sprouted nuts, seeds, pulses and grains are easier to digest. The process removes phytic acid (a protective enzyme), which not only causes digestive discomfort – including gas and bloating – but can also rob your body of nutrients.

WHY SPROUT?

Sprouts are alive, rich in oxygen and one of the most nourishing foods you can eat. Once sprouted, grains, seeds and beans have fifteen to thirty per cent more protein. They also offer up to ten times more B-vitamins then their non-sprouted counterparts, as well as more vitamins C, E and K, beta-carotene, calcium, phosphorus and iron.

WHAT TO SPROUT

Seeds
Beans
Pulses
Grains

SOAKING

Place about 100g seeds, beans, pulses or grains in a bowl and pour over enough water to fully cover. Add 1 tbsp apple cider vinegar, which helps the outer layers break down, thus aiding germination, then cover the bowl with a clean cloth. Soak at room temperature for 2–12 hours depending on the size of the seed: 2–4 hours is enough for smaller seeds, 5–10 hours for medium-sized and 11–12 hours for larger (see table, right).

GERMINATION

Drain the seeds, beans, pulses or grains into a fine mesh sieve, or a muslin cloth-lined colander. Rinse well. Set the sieve or cloth-lined colander back over the bowl. Dampen the cloth you used to cover the soaking seeds, beans, pulses or grains initially and use it to cover the bowl, to help the drained seeds retain their moisture. Keep at room temperature, in a cool place out of direct sunlight and rinsing once or twice every day, until the seeds, beans, pulses or grains start to germinate: they'll produce little tails when they do.

STORING AND EATING

As soon as they're sprouted, ensure they are fully dry, then store them in the refrigerator and eat within three days. They're delicious whizzed into smoothies (1–2 tbsp sprouted quinoa is delicious in a Winter spa smoothie, see page 46), used for porridge, soups, stews and risottos, or as a final nutritious flourish to scatter over finished dishes.

AVOID! (HARD TO SPROUT)

Brazil nuts
Cashew nuts
Flaxseed
Macadamia nuts
Pecans
Pine nuts
Walnuts

SPROUTING TIMETABLE

SPROUT	SOAKING	SPROUTING
Alfalfa	4 hours	2 days
Almonds	12 hours	12 hours
Amaranth	2 hours	2–3 days
Barley	7 hours	2 days
Broccoli	4 hours	2 days
Buckwheat (raw groats)	12 hours	1–2 days
Chickpeas	12 hours	12 hours
Fenugreek	8 hours	3–5 days
Kale	4 hours	2 days
Lentils	8 hours	12 hours
Millet	8 hours	2–3 days
Mung beans	12 hours	3–5 days
Oat groats	6 hours	2–3 days
Pumpkin	12 hours	2–3 days
Quinoa	2 hours	1–2 days
Radish	4 hours	2 days
Red cabbage	4 hours	2 days
Rice	8 hours	3–5 days
Sesame	4 hours	1–2 days
Spelt, rye and wheat	8 hours	2–3 days
Sunflower	2 hours	2–3 days

Four winter salad leaves to grow

Sure, growing winter salads gives you the perkiest, crispest, freshest leaves. They're also more nutritious. But that's not why you should do it... or not entirely.

The simple art of nurturing and harvesting your own leaves has deeper benefits. It's calming. It's a mindful way to engage with what you put in your body. And it's cheaper and you avoid all the horrible plastic.

You don't need a garden, or even a window box, to grow these. You can literally nurture them on your kitchen table, so long as they have access to fleeting moments of winter sunshine. Once you've got your space sorted, salad leaves grow within just thirty or forty days of planting. For the same price as a bag of salad leaves, you can buy a pack of seeds that could keep you in lettuce permanently for two years. Here are my favourite cut-and-come-again varieties for winter.

KOMATSUNA These fan-like leaves look like mini versions of pak choi. A form of wild turnip, the hardy green is sometimes referred to as 'Japanese mustard spinach', although it isn't spinach but a member of the brassica family. It is a biennial that is tolerant of very cold temperatures, so can be sown outside in autumn for winter growth, or in a patio or windowsill pot.

MIZUNA Another Japanese green, mizuna is a versatile, leafy crop with a mild mustard flavour similar to rocket, but slightly more bitter. It's packed with vitamins A, C and K, as well as calcium and iron. It grows well indoors in winter, whether in a greenhouse, polytunnel or a small pot on the kitchen windowsill.

MUSTARD 'Red frills' is one of the prettiest winter salads to grow, with feathery, softly serrated leaves. They have a mild spicy note followed by a deliciously odd fresh-boiled-new-potato flavour. You can sow the seeds little and often and eat as microgreens, or let them grow on a few centimetres and use in a baby leaf salad. Larger leaves are great in stir-fries.

RADICCHIO Known as the jewel of the winter garden, sculptural crowns of red radicchio always shine on the plate and the palate, too. While they have a bitter note, the cold of winter also teases out an irresistible sweetness. Sow in late summer for winter harvesting. You can grow radicchio in pots, as well, for small, tender heads.

BITTERSWEET SALAD

Winter leaves tend to have more robust flavours. Think of bitter radicchio – with its blowsy, cold-tolerant leaves – and all the mustardy varieties such as the peppery feather-like leaves of mizuna and nose-tingly mustard leaves with wasabi-like heat. Add a few punchy wild leaves such as dandelion, chicory and goosegrass and you've got an even more healthy bowlful, as wild leaves add more nutritional diversity which has a strongly positive impact on the gut microbiome.

Here, a calming dressing for these feisty flavours is made with the soft sweetness of a whole clementine. Whipped with linseed or olive oil, the mildly acidic juice emulsifies into the perfect thick, creamy coat for winter leaves.

SERVES 2–4

100g winter salad leaves (see recipe introduction)
4 tbsp broccoli, radish, or kale sprouts (see page 66)
handful of foraged leaves, such as dandelion (optional,
   see recipe introduction)
1 clementine
4 tbsp linseed oil, or olive oil
sea salt and freshly ground black pepper
Digestive dukkah, or Mushroom furikake (see pages 226 and 224),
   to serve (optional)

Wash the winter salad leaves, sprouts and foraged leaves, if using.

Cut the whole skin-on clementine into bite-sized pieces (cut it in half, then quarter each half). Remove any pips. Blend the cut clementine with the linseed oil or olive oil and a pinch of salt. It should render into a thick and creamy dressing.

Toss the washed salad mix with the dressing and arrange on plates, or in a bowl. Season with black pepper and finish with a dusting of dukkah or furikake, if you like.

MUSHROOM AND BLACK GARLIC PATÉ

Two immune-boosting wonders come together in a tastebud-tantalising paté. Black garlic has powerful antibiotic properties, but it selects and targets harmful bacteria, while leaving the good guys intact. Mushrooms are rich in macronutrients such as vitamins D and B6, which further support the immune system.

I love having this paté in the refrigerator. It's the perfect base for a quick lunch, or pre-dinner nibbles, or you can use it as a sauce (thin it out with a little stock) for pasta. It's great on Seedy crackers (see page 41), which is how we shot it for the photograph here.

It is just as good made using rehydrated dried mushrooms: 50g dried mushrooms should give you 200g once rehydrated.

SERVES 2–4

200g cooked mushrooms (L'escargot mushrooms, see page 86, work well, as do dried mushrooms, see recipe introduction)
100g walnuts, or hazelnuts
2 tbsp black garlic cloves
2 tbsp chopped herbs, or wild greens such as thyme leaves or three-cornered leek
1 lemon
2–3 tbsp olive oil, plus more to store
sea salt and freshly ground black pepper

Blend the mushrooms, nuts, black garlic and herbs or wild greens, or pulse-blend everything in a food processor, until you have a coarse paste. Season generously with black pepper, a pinch of salt and the finely grated zest of the lemon along with a squeeze of its juice. Blend in enough olive oil to bring it all together, to taste.

You can eat this straight away, or pack it into a jar and cover with a layer of olive oil, whereupon it will keep happily in the refrigerator for a week.

CLASSIC SAUERKRAUT

What's lovely about this basic canvas is that you can make so many variations simply by using different seasonal cabbages. You can also change up the herbs and spices, adding grated ginger or horseradish, or swapping the apple for pear or quince if you have some stored, for instance. Each of these subtle changes results in a kraut unique to the moment you make it, which is, therefore, like edible poetry. You will need a 500g jar with a lid.

MAKES ABOUT 500G

½ cabbage (white, green or red)
1 apple (optional)
1 teaspoon caraway, cumin or fennel seeds, or finely grated root ginger
  or horseradish (optional)
sea salt

Reserve a couple of outer large leaves from the cabbage. Thinly shred the cabbage, including the core. Coarsely grate the apple, keeping the skin on but discarding the core. Weigh the cabbage and apple and calculate 2 per cent its weight in salt; so for every 100g cabbage and apple, add 2g salt.

Pop the cabbage, apple and measured salt into a big bowl. Add the flavouring seeds or roots, if using. Get your hands in there and massage and scrunch the cabbage for a minute or so, until you feel all the salt has dissolved. Alternatively, you can simply mix the salt through, cover the bowl and let it sit for at least 30 minutes, or up to overnight, in which time the salt will have dissolved and drawn out some of the cabbage and apple's juices.

Spoon the juicy cabbage mix into the jar, adding it little by little and packing down each layer as you go. It's important to exclude as much air as possible during this process. Pour any leftover brine in the bowl over the cabbage. Use the large reserved cabbage leaves to cover the compacted cabbage, trimming and bending them to fit over the top. Tuck the sides of the leaf cap in around the edges as much as you can. Press the leaf cap down until there's enough brine to come to the top of the jar. If you don't have enough, make extra by mixing 50ml water with 2g sea salt and pouring it into the jar.

Screw an airtight lid on the jar and place it on a plate to catch any juices that bubble over during fermentation. Transfer it to a dry spot, at room temperature, out of direct sunlight. Twist the lid open if the jar is hissing, to release any building gases. Check the cabbage is still covered with brine. If it isn't, add a little fresh brine by sprinkling a pinch of salt into the jar and pouring in enough filtered or mineral water to come right to the top.

Let it ferment for 2 weeks. You can tuck in straight away, keep it fermenting at room temperature – which develops the flavour further – or pop into the fridge. Once opened, refrigerate and eat within 6 weeks. It keeps for 1 year at room temperature in a dark, cool place, as long as it's covered with brine.

LEMON AND THYME CELERIKRAUT

This kraut reminds me of celeriac rémoulade and it makes a completely delicious Christmas feasting companion: it's wonderful with smoked trout, roast turkey, goose or venison, mushroom wellington and so much more.

MAKES ABOUT 2 × 200G JARS

½ celeriac
1 pear
2 garlic cloves, finely grated
finely grated zest of 1 lemon
leaves from 2–3 thyme sprigs
6–8 bay leaves
sea salt

Carve the woody peel from the celeriac using a knife (I find most peelers suffer with this job), then quarter and coarsely grate it. Grate the pear down to the core, keeping the skin on.

Weigh the celeriac and pear and calculate 2 per cent its weight in salt; so for every 100g celeriac and pear, add 2g salt. Get your hands in there and massage and scrunch the mixture for a minute or so, until you feel all the salt has dissolved. Alternatively, you can simply mix the salt through, cover the bowl and let it sit for at least 30 minutes, or up to overnight, in which time the salt will have dissolved and drawn out some of the celeriac's juices.

Add the garlic, lemon zest and thyme leaves and fold through the mix.

Pack the mix into a jar, adding it little by little and packing down each layer as you go. It's important to exclude as much air as possible during this process. Add the leftover brine in the bowl. Arrange the bay leaves over the top, to help keep the mix covered, overlapping the leaves to fully cover. Press the leaf cap down until there's enough brine to come to the top of the jar. If you don't have enough, make extra by mixing 50ml water with 2g sea salt and pouring it into the jar. Screw an airtight lid on the jar and place it on a plate to catch any juices that bubble over during fermentation.

Transfer it to a dry spot, at room temperature, out of direct sunlight. Take off the lid once a day to release accumulating gases and to check the celeriac is still covered with brine. If it isn't, add a little fresh brine by sprinkling a pinch of salt in and topping up with enough filtered or mineral water to come fully to the top of the jar.

Let it ferment for 2 weeks. Smell and taste: once it's tender and tangy enough for you, it's ready to eat. Tuck in straight away, or store in the refrigerator in a sealed, sterilised jar (see page 188) until you're ready to eat it. As long as it's covered in brine and the lid is airtight, it will keep for months. Should it start to look or smell off, discard it.

CELERIAC SEVILLE CEVICHE

The first time I made this, I'd invited one of my food heroes (and now colleagues) Hugh Fearnley-Whittingstall for dinner. I was going to make classic fish ceviche, but the fishmonger was closed and I had ceviche on the brain... so I bravely improvised. It has since become a winter kitchen staple of mine. You can't beat the simplicity and I'm always surprised at how quickly it disappears: it's often half eaten before I get it to the table. It's also hugely versatile. I serve it as a side dish to all manner of cuisines, from Lebanese mezze, to hearty English comfort food such as roast lamb.

SERVES 4

½ celeriac
2 Seville oranges, 1 blood orange, or ½ grapefruit
1 tbsp olive oil
pinch of rosemary flowers and/or small leaves (optional)
sea salt and freshly ground black pepper

Carve the woody peel from the celeriac using a knife (I find most peelers suffer with this job). Once peeled, carve the flesh as finely as you can, into bite-sized wisps. I use a large knife, but you can use a mandoline, if you have one, the shaving side of a box grater, or a veg peeler.

Pile the celeriac wisps into a bowl. Finely grate the zest of the citrus over, you want a good 1–2 tsp. Dust a little salt over the celeriac slivers. Squeeze the citrus juice on top, using a sieve to catch the pips, then toss to mix. Let the celeriac marinate for at least 30 minutes, or up to a day in the refrigerator.

Arrange on a plate. Finish with a drizzle of olive oil, a pinch more salt, a good hit of black pepper and a dusting of rosemary flowers and/or small rosemary leaves, if you have them.

SARA'S SWEDISH PIZZA SALAD

The title of this recipe might leave you a touch baffled. I'll elaborate. One of my dearest friends is Swedish and her name is Sara. She lived with me for a short spell and one of the many delicious things she made during her stay was this simple salad, intriguingly nicknamed 'pizza salad'. In Sweden, this is what you are served alongside a dough-crusted pie. My son and I went to visit Sara in Sweden recently, ordered pizza one night (the most incredible wild mushroom and forest fruit combination) and – ta-da! – we experienced the magic of pizza salad, which is like an unfermented sauerkraut, or a pressed slaw, if you prefer. As well as with pizza, it's also brilliant with grilled fish, falafel and houmous, roast lamb, or served as part of a selection of veg sides as a mezze. I love it. Another illustration of winter veg in the purest, most delicious format.

When you eat brassicas raw, you benefit from sulforaphane, a chemical in raw cruciferous veg that calms inflammation in the body and can block the mutations that lead to cancer (see page 302).

SERVES 4

½ white cabbage (or you can use green and/or red)
2 tbsp olive oil, or as needed
2 tbsp white wine vinegar, or as needed
1 tsp dried or fresh oregano, basil or dill leaves, or as needed
sea salt and freshly ground black pepper

Finely shred the cabbage and toss into a bowl.

Mix the olive oil and vinegar with the herb of choice and a good pinch of salt and pepper. Drizzle the dressing over the shredded cabbage. Mix the dressing through and, using clean hands, squeeze and knead the leaves well to release their juices.

Taste, adjust with one of the dressing ingredients, if needed, and top up with more pepper and salt if you like. While you can serve this straight away, the traditional recipe suggests placing a heavy bowl or plate on top of the salad to weigh it down and letting it marinate and soften for up to 12 hours in the refrigerator (or it will happily keep for 5–6 days).

Nourishing salad dressings

You can't go wrong with a classic French vinaigrette and it's a brilliant way of tucking healthy fats into a meal, as well as including vitamin C-rich ingredients which boost the body's intake of iron from leafy greens.

A classic vinaigrette contains three parts fat to one part acid. Therefore, you would whisk 30ml olive oil with 10ml vinegar. But these rules are flexible.

The oil can be swapped for a fat such as nut butter, dairy such as kefir or cheese, or a vegan equivalent.

The acid can be classic vinegar or citrus juice, or you can use a purée of acidic fruits such as persimmons or clementines (see page 68).

Additional elements to include in a great salad dressing are a hint of sweetness, a touch of salt and the pungency of mustard. Mixing the mustard with the vinegar before whisking in the oil can help stabilise the dressing, as well as give a peppery heat. For a sweeter dressing, consider finishing with a drop of maple syrup, date syrup or purée. You can apply creativity by blending in herbs or spices. And always remember to season with salt and pepper.

PERFECT TIMING

Wait to dress your salad until just before serving, otherwise it will wilt!

SALAD DRESSING INGREDIENTS

ACID

Vinegar:
apple cider
balsamic
infused (see pages 200–202)
red wine
rice
white wine

Sauerkraut brine

Kimchi brine

Pickle juice

Citrus:
bergamot
clementine
finger lime
kumquat
lemon
lime
orange
satsuma
Seville orange
... add the zest, too, it has natural oils which makes the dressing creamier

Kombucha

FAT

Oil:
blackberry seed
hazelnut
hemp
linseed
olive
pumpkin seed
rapeseed
sesame
walnut

Nut and seed butter:
almond
cashew
peanut
pumpkin seed
tahini

Kefir or yogurt (they can stand alone as a dressing, as they're both fat and acid)

SEASONINGS

Sweetness:
dates
honey
maple syrup
molasses

Herbs:
lavender
oregano
rosemary
sage
thyme

Spices:
cardamom
caraway
chilli
coriander
cumin
fennel
ginger

Garlic

Mustard

Sea salt:
garlic
herb
seaweed
smoked

LEMON VINAIGRETTE

This is a classic vinaigrette, featuring lemon juice in place of vinegar, but you can easily jazz it up by using different vinegars, including homemade vinegars infused with herbs such as thyme stalks (or see pages 200–202). You can also swap out olive oil for any nut or seed oil (and see the table, opposite, to get ideas about some other fun combinations). It's worth emphasising once more that the benefit of pairing this deliciously tangy dressing with green leaves is that the vitamin C in the lemon helps your body to absorb more iron from the greens.

SERVES 4

finely grated zest of 1 lemon, plus 2 tbsp lemon juice
6 tbsp olive oil
1 small garlic clove, or ½ larger garlic clove, finely grated
1 tsp honey, or maple syrup (optional)
sea salt and freshly ground black pepper

Whisk the lemon zest and juice and oil together with the garlic, honey or maple syrup, if using, and a pinch of salt and pepper until thick and creamy. Alternatively, you can shake everything together in a lidded jam jar. It will keep for 2 weeks in the refrigerator.

COUGH REMEDY CARROTS

While you could add honey (and arguably – my mum would have been in favour – a drop of whisky) to the mix, this salad features those top cough remedy ingredients of lemon, garlic and thyme. It's another deliciously simple mix that packs a flavour punch and helps you stay happy and well from head to toe, with a special nod to your throat. Miles better than cough syrup!

SERVES 4

2 large carrots, or 4 smaller carrots
1 large lemon, or 2 smaller lemons
1 garlic clove, finely chopped or grated
1 tbsp fresh or dried thyme leaves
2 tbsp olive oil, or flaxseed oil
sea salt and freshly ground black pepper

With a veg peeler, run down the length of each carrot to create thin ribbons. Tumble them into a large mixing bowl. Grate in the zest of the lemon(s). Add the garlic, thyme and juice from the lemon(s) with a pinch of salt and pepper.

Toss everything together and let the carrots soften in the lemon juice for at least 15 minutes at room temperature, or in the refrigerator for up to a day.

Drizzle with the oil before serving.

MAPLE MISO ROAST CAULIFLOWER

Cooking a whole cauliflower in a lidded pot steams it into a deliciously tender state, which is the perfect base for lapping up the sweet and salty flavours of this maple miso glaze. Flashed under the grill, it then caramelises, creating a Japanese barbecue sauce-like glaze. The cauliflower becomes soft and almost 'pullable' like pork shoulder, albeit a plant-based brassica version. It's truly delicious and looks impressive.

SERVES 4

1 cauliflower
2 tsp (any) oil, butter, or ghee (for homemade, see page 214)
4 tbsp miso
2 tbsp maple syrup
thumb of root ginger, finely grated (about 2 tbsp)

To serve (optional)
1 tbsp sesame seeds, or Mushroom furikake (see page 224)
pinch of chilli flakes

Preheat the oven to 200°C/190°C fan.

Trim the larger leaves from the cauliflower (treat them like cabbage leaves and add to Sara's Swedish pizza salad, see page 76, or to a homemade kimchi or kraut, see pages 206 and 72–73).

Lightly oil the base of a lidded pot large enough to hold the cauliflower with 1 tsp of the oil, butter or ghee.

Place the cauliflower in the pot, place the lid on top and slide into the oven for 45–60 minutes or until the cauliflower is tender right the way through. While it cooks, mix the miso, maple syrup and ginger.

Remove the lid from the cauliflower pot. Lightly oil a baking dish with the remaining oil, butter or ghee and transfer the cauliflower to the baking dish. Brush the miso glaze all over the cauliflower. Return to the oven. Crank the heat up to 220°C/210°C fan and roast for a further 15–20 minutes or until the cauliflower is toasty and caramelised.

Finish with a dusting of sesame seeds, furikake, and/or chilli flakes, if you like.

LIME AND GINGER PARSNIPS

There are so many wonderful flavours to partner with parsnips. Seaweed and sesame are wonderful, with a finishing hint of soy sauce or tamari. Lemon zest, a squeeze of the juice, a pinch of thyme and a hit of black pepper also serve the earthy root well. But this recipe is simplicity at its best. The fragrant tang of lime and the gentle warmth of ginger bring subtle Thai notes, contrasting with the caramelised sugars that are teased out during the process of roasting parsnips. I can happily eat an entire bowl of these on their own, but they're also wonderful with roasted mackerel, or served with rice and salad.

You can finish this with a dusting of sesame seeds, finely chopped coriander or Mushroom furikake (see page 224), but I like the elegance of the dish in its purest form.

SERVES 4

1kg parsnips, well scrubbed
2 tbsp coconut oil, or ghee (for homemade, see page 214)
thumb of root ginger
2 limes
sea salt and freshly ground black pepper

Preheat the oven to 200°C/190°C fan. Place a baking tray on a high shelf in the oven to heat up.

Cut the parsnips into chunks, 5–6cm long and about 2cm thick, keeping the peel on as it has so much flavour and nutritional value.

Remove the tray from the oven. Add the coconut oil or ghee and the parsnips. Season with salt and pepper. Fold through the oil or ghee and slide into the oven to roast for 30–40 minutes or until golden and tender.

Finely grate about 2 tbsp ginger over the just-cooked parsnips. Grate over the zest of both limes and squeeze over the juice. Mix well, then taste and add more salt and pepper, as needed.

L'ESCARGOT MUSHROOMS

The name of this recipe comes from the remarkable resemblance to snails that the pairing of garlic parsley butter and these roasted mushrooms evokes. They are delicious with Parisian omelette crêpes (see page 36), served alongside steak or piled on toast. Any leftovers can be whizzed into Mushroom and black garlic paté (see page 70); you may even want to scale up the recipe so you can have enough left for paté.

SERVES 2-4

1 garlic clove, finely minced or grated
10g flat leaf parsley, finely chopped
50g butter, softened
1 lemon
400g chestnut mushrooms, or wild mushrooms
sea salt and freshly ground black pepper

Preheat the oven to 200°C/190°C fan. Set a large roasting tray in the oven to heat up.

Blend the garlic and parsley into the soft butter until smooth. Grate in the zest of the lemon and season well with salt and pepper, then whizz to mix thoroughly. Taste, add a little lemon juice and more seasoning, if needed. Chill until ready to use.

Quarter the mushrooms if they're large (leave smaller mushrooms whole), or tear them into bite-sized pieces if using wild mushrooms. Arrange them in the preheated roasting tray with a pinch of salt, in a single layer. Roast for 10–15 minutes, adding no oil or butter at this stage (you want to cook the water out of the mushrooms first).

Once the mushrooms are nicely tender and a little shrivelled, swirl in the garlic butter. Slide back into the oven, allowing the mushrooms to cook in the butter for a minute or so, until the butter is melted and a bright green.

Season with a little more salt and pepper, if needed, then serve warm.

BAY-ROASTED BEETS

Blushing beetroots are a bundle of winter-protective nutrients such as betalains, which contain powerful antioxidant, anti-inflammatory and detoxifying properties. I love beetroot in just about every guise: raw, pickled, smoked, fermented... This is my favourite way to prepare them and probably the easiest (apart from raw, but that can be messy). Bay pairs so beautifully with beetroot, offering a subtle pine-like fragrance to the roasted roots. You can skip the yogurt or labneh if you're dairy free, or swap it for a plant-based option, or have these roasted beets, once cut into bite-sized chunks, simply tossed in a Lemon vinaigrette (see page 79). They are delicious served alongside Wild and sprouted falafel with cardamom-lime tahini (see page 64).

SERVES 4

1–2 large bay sprigs (8–12 leaves)
2 large beetroots, or 4 smaller beetroots, cleaned
250g Greek yogurt, or Kefir labneh (see page 256)
1 garlic clove, finely grated
1 tsp caraway seeds, or cumin seeds, plus more to serve
1 tbsp olive oil, or linseed oil
sea salt and freshly ground black pepper

To serve
handful of herbs, or winter leaves
Digestive dukkah (see page 226, optional)

Preheat the oven to 200°C/190°C fan.

Arrange the bay in a lidded ovenproof pot. Set the beetroots on top, skins on. Bake in the preheated oven for 1 hour or until the beetroot is tender right the way through (pierce with a small, sharp knife to check).

Allow the beetroot to cool. Mix the yogurt or labneh with the grated garlic and the caraway or cumin seeds. Season with salt and pepper to taste. Spoon the yogurt into a serving dish or on a platter.

Brush off any tougher bits of beetroot peel and trim off the knobbly tops. Halve the beetroots and cut into bite-sized pieces.

Place the beetroots on the yogurt. Finish with a drizzling of the olive oil or linseed oil. Season with salt and pepper and finish with herbs or winter leaves, or try a sprinkling of Digestive dukkah.

COCONUT CURRIED SWEDE CAKES

In the depths of Wales on a cold winter's day, I made a batch of these
when I was catering for a private client. The client was on a strict diet that
excluded grains, among many other things, so I made these in place of
bread, to have alongside soup. They went down a treat, and always do when
I serve them to people who think they don't like eating swede. Surprisingly,
the spices and coconut are the perfect match for the robust winter root.

MAKES 12–16 BITE-SIZED
(FALAFEL-LIKE) CAKES

1 swede, peeled and cut into 2–3cm dice
2–3 tbsp coconut oil
1 onion, finely chopped
2 garlic cloves, finely chopped
1 tbsp ground cumin, or Winter five spice (see page 230)
thumb of root ginger, finely grated
thumb of root turmeric, finely grated
pinch of cayenne pepper (optional)
handful of finely chopped parsley leaves, or coriander leaves
sea salt and freshly ground black pepper

Preheat the oven to 200°C/190°C fan and place a large roasting tray inside
to warm up. Toss the swede with salt and pepper and tumble into the warm
roasting tin with 1 tbsp of the coconut oil. Cook for 25 minutes, or until
golden and tender.

Add the onion to the swede and roast for a further 10 minutes. Remove from
the oven and fold the garlic through.

Measure the spices and stir them into the swede.

Blend the roasted swede, onion, garlic and spices in a food processor with
the parsley or coriander until fairly smooth. You'll have a few lumpy bits of
swede, but that's fine, they add texture.

Form into golf ball-sized chunks, then press them a little so they form flat
falafel-like cakes. (If you have more mix than you need, freeze the rest at
this point. Defrost fully before cooking.)

To cook, shallow-fry the cakes in a frying pan in the remaining oil until
golden on each side, adding more oil as you cook, if needed.

LAZY ONIONS

My eyes just can't cope with chopping onions. If I need a good cry, finely slicing a kilo of onions will get the tears flowing. If I don't, then one way to avoid it – while reaping all the delicious benefits of caramelised onions – is to roast them whole. It's one of the laziest things you can do in the kitchen that yields such delicious results. All you have to do is turn the oven on, tumble whole onions into a dish, slide them into the oven and let time and temperature work their magic. After about an hour (or less for smaller onions), the sweet tender flesh will just pop out of the papery skins, giving you a caramelised allium bulb. A little seasoning and a drizzle of oil is all you really need to transform them into a delicious side dish. Once made, enjoy them as a side dish for roast lamb or beef, alongside a spread of dips and salads, or tossed with noodles and microgreens.

SERVES 4

4 larger red or white onions, or 8 smaller ones, or 12 shallots
3 tbsp olive oil, butter, or ghee (for homemade, see page 214)
12–15 sage leaves
sea salt

Preheat the oven to 200°C/190°C fan.

Arrange the alliums in a roasting tray and slide into the oven for 30 minutes for shallots, 45 minutes for smaller onions, or 1 hour for larger onions. They are ready when the skins are blistered and the onions have collapsed a little and are starting to burst from their skins. The juices will have spilled from the onions, caramelised and burned around the outside of the onion skin, which might not look so great, but means that inside the onion has caramelised and the flavours have intensified, making them sweetly delicious.

While they cook, gently warm the oil, butter or ghee in a frying pan. Add the sage with a pinch of salt and cook over a medium heat until crisp.

Once cooked, let the onions cool slightly, then press them out of their skins and drizzle the sage-y oil, butter or ghee over. Serve warm, dotting the crispy sage leaves over the top.

TURKISH TAHINI GREENS

Whip up this little number and soon you'll be pairing the tahini dressing with just about everything...

SERVES 4–6

4 tbsp tahini
4 tbsp olive oil, plus more to serve
2 tbsp red wine vinegar
2 tbsp water
½ tsp ground cumin
finely grated zest and juice of 2 lemons
3 garlic cloves, finely minced or grated
4 large handfuls of dark leafy greens (kale, cavolo nero or spinach)
sea salt and freshly ground black pepper
pinch of chilli flakes, or chilli powder, to serve (optional)

Bring a pot or kettle of water to the boil.

In a bowl, whisk the tahini, olive oil, red wine vinegar, measured water, ground cumin and the zest and juice of 1 of the lemons. Swirl in 1 of the garlic cloves (finely minced or grated first, of course). Season to taste with salt and pepper and add a little more lemon juice, if you fancy.

Tug the softer leafy greens from their woody stalks and roughly chop. If you're using cavolo nero, keep the smaller leaves whole, as they're so pretty.

Stuff the leaves into a pot. Pour enough hot water over just to cover and swirl through. Simmer for 1 minute or until they are a bright and glossy green, then drain and rinse.

Fold the remaining garlic through the warm greens, adding it little by little and tasting as you go. Season well.

Gloss with oil. Add a good grating of lemon zest (save a bit for serving) and a generous squeeze of lemon juice. Taste and tweak as needed.

Swirl the tahini mixture on to a plate or into a bowl so it's totally covering the base. Pile the greens on top. Finish with another gloss of oil, lemon zest, sea salt, pepper and a little chilli, if you like.

Guide to growing microgreens

Microgreens encompass a broad spectrum: not just greens and herbs, but also other vegetables. In essence, microgreens are the first shoots of edible plants that include the stem, the cotyledons (or seed leaves) and the first set of true leaves, so about the first 5–6cm of growth of a plant.

Some refer to them as 'vegetable confetti', as microgreens encompass the depth and breadth of all veggies from alfalfa, broccoli, kale, spinach or watercress and extending to non-green veggies such as beetroot, radishes and sweetcorn, even to grains such as quinoa, as well as all manner of herbs including basil, coriander, dill and parsley.

Not only do microgreens look brilliant on a plate of food – adding extra visual zest and appeal, as well as an intense flavour boost – they also enrich the nutritional profile enormously, offering essential nutrients and more.

Research has shown that microgreens contain considerably higher concentrations of vitamins, up to forty times more, than their mature plant counterparts. Beyond the bounty of nutritional benefits, microgreens are also easy to grow at home or even inside your own kitchen.

FIVE MINI LEAVES I LOVE

BASIL   'Dark opal', or purple, basil is especially delicious and I find it much easier to grow mini leaves rather than full-sized basil plants. It has a lovely aniseed note with a hint of cinnamon.

CORIANDER   Citrusy and fragrant, coriander features prominently in a number of cuisines, from Mexican to Thai. It's also hugely medicinal. One notable quality is its ability to help the body expel toxins from heavy metals, such as mercury fillings (see page 302).

DILL   The willowy wisps and citrus hints of dill add a touch of Scandinavia to dishes. I love garnishing Kefir labneh, or Mushroom and black garlic paté (see pages 256 and 70) with baby dill leaves.

PEA SHOOTS   One of the first things I started growing in my kitchen. Even though the seeds are much larger than dainty herb seeds, peas germinate quickly and you should have a crop of shoots within a week of sowing. They add the hopeful flavour of spring to winter salads.

SUNFLOWER GREENS   Deep green and rich in chlorophyll, sunflower is among the healthiest microgreens you can grow. The texture is nutty and the shoots add brilliant crunch to a salad, but are equally wonderful whizzed into Winter spa smoothies (see page 46).

START WITH THE SEEDS

Beginners often start by growing one type of seed, such as broccoli, buckwheat, cabbage, cauliflower, chia, mustard or sunflower – among the easiest-to-grow varieties of microgreens – in a single container. (You can easily grow different seeds in several containers and mix your microgreens after harvesting.)

You can also find seeds for salad mixes, and specially selected microgreen mixes that combine greens with similar growth rates, compatible flavours and beautiful colours, including reds and purples alongside greens. Since they were created with grower success in mind, they're a good choice for beginners.

If your climate is suitable, microgreens can also be grown outdoors in the garden, under shade. As with all fragile seedlings, you'll need to protect them from weather extremes and drying winds, not to mention hungry garden pests.

STEP-BY-STEP

Start with a warm, sunny windowsill (direct sunlight from a south-facing window is ideal) and a small, clean container. Something measuring roughly 15 × 8cm and 5–6cm deep is ideal. You can easily find these online, or create your own using recycled materials. If your chosen container doesn't have built-in drainage, poke a few drainage holes in the bottom. Then, prepare to plant:

Read the seed packet to see if there are any special instructions for your chosen variety.

Cover the bottom of the container with up to 5cm of moistened potting soil or mix. Flatten and level it with your hand or a small piece of cardboard, taking care not to over-compress the soil.

Scatter seeds evenly on top of the soil. Press gently into the soil using your hand or the cardboard.

Cover the seeds with a thin layer of soil. Dampen the surface with a mister.

While waiting for sprouts to appear, usually within three to seven days, use the mister once or twice daily to keep the soil moist but not wet.

Once seeds have sprouted, continue to mist once or twice a day.

Microgreens need about four hours daily of direct sunlight to thrive. In winter months, some may need even more. Leggy, pale greens are a sign that your microgreens are not getting enough sunlight.

HARVESTING

Depending on the type of seeds you've selected, the microgreens will be ready to harvest two to three weeks after planting. Look for the first set of 'true leaves' as a sign of readiness. Then grab your scissors and snip the greens just above the soil line.

STORING AND SERVING

To serve, wash the microgreens with water and dry with kitchen paper or in a salad spinner. Harvest and serve them immediately for the freshest flavour, adding them to soups, salads, sandwiches or main dishes. Store any remaining cut microgreens in a lidded container in the refrigerator. They will keep for a week, though it's best not to wash them until right before serving, as water can make them deteriorate more quickly.

ROAST SQUASH WITH KIMCHI BUTTER

As much as I mourn the end of lazy, hazy, hot summer days, the arrival of the autumn's first golden globes stirs my culinary brain into a frenzy of delight. I love squash and the joy of growing and buying it is that most varieties are made for storing to provide winter fuel. I get greedy and buy loads, with one always ready and waiting.

My knee-jerk method for preparing squash is the simplest: just halve (if small), quarter (if medium) or cut into chunky wedges (if large) and roast until tender right the way through and caramelised around the edges. From there, you can blend it into a soup (unless the skin is really tough, you can eat it or blend it into the mix), or mash it with butter or coconut oil to accompany roast hogget or provide a bed for pan-fried scallops.

Or just drizzle something delicious over the top, like this umami-rich, palate-pleasing mix of kimchi brine and butter.

SERVES 2–4 (DEPENDING ON THE SIZE OF THE SQUASH)

1 squash (a medium Red Kuri is my favourite here)
1 tbsp coconut oil, or ghee (for homemade, see page 214)
4 tbsp butter, softened
4 tbsp kimchi brine (from a jar of kimchi)
sea salt and freshly ground black pepper
sprinkle of microgreens or sprouts (optional, see pages 94–95 and 66), to serve

Preheat the oven to 200°C/190°C fan. Set a large roasting dish in the oven to heat up.

Cut the squash in half if small, in quarters if medium or into 4–5cm thick wedges if large. Scoop out the seeds (use them to test your sprouting skills, see page 66, or roast them, or compost them). Put the oil or ghee in the heated dish. Arrange in the squash, coating it in the fat and leaving it cut side down, or on one of the cut sides, if in wedges. Roast for 30 minutes.

Remove the pan from the oven, flip the squash to the other side (or cut side up if you have halves). Roast for a further 15–30 minutes, or until fully tender and visibly caramelised around the cut edges.

While it cooks or slightly cools, blend the butter and kimchi brine together: mix it in a bowl with a spoon, or use a stick blender or food processor for a lighter whipped result. Dot the kimchi butter over the squash, to taste. If you have extra, the butter will keep nicely in the refrigerator for 1 week, or in the freezer for 1 year. It's worth making extra to have on hand for other things such as fish (it makes an instant sauce), or to be tossed with noodles or rice. Serve sprinkled with microgreens or sprouts, if you like.

STOCKS,

SOUPS

AND
STEWS

*'Come to me, those whose stomachs
ache, and I will restore you.'*

In a poetic vein, soup can be seen as a vehicle to manoeuvre one from a recovering state of winter into a resurgent spring with renewed spirit and vivacity.

Engraved above the door of the world's first restaurant was the invitation, on the previous page, to imbibe consommés or *restaurants*. In 18th-century France, a *restaurant* referred to a bouillon. Literally, the word means 'to restore'.

At the time, the streets of Paris were full of vendors selling soup. Prescriptions included the iconic French onion soup with its rich beef bouillon base. Wealthy fashionistas lapped them up, deeming these broths to be near-magical elixirs. In 1767, legend has it that a man named Boulanger transferred his streetside soup stall to a cosy indoor space on Rue des Poulies, giving birth to the first restaurant as we know it today. And it all started with soup.

HEAT AND BONES

The alchemy that is stirred when ingredients are infused in water over warming flames has entranced humans since the beginning of time. Bone broths were one of the first foods cooked over fire. Neolithic man is thought to have harnessed the power of heat to draw nutrients from bones, in earthen pits lined with animal skins. To heat the water, they'd drop in stones that had been left over a fire to become red-hot. These would slowly transform the liquid into a comforting, hydrating bowl of sustenance.

GUT HEALING VEG STOCK

This is a brilliantly complex yet easy vegetable stock that has the depth of flavour and golden colour of a good chicken stock. The prune, if you have one, lends body and healing properties. It makes a brilliant base for any or all of the recipes that follow in this chapter, so it's worth simmering up a double amount and stashing it in the freezer for other dishes.

MAKES 1 LITRE

1 large carrot
1 celery stick, or 1 slice of celeriac
1 onion and/or leek
2 garlic cloves
12g dried mushrooms, or 50g fresh mushrooms
1 prune (optional)
small bunch of thyme and/or 3–4 bay leaves
2 slices of root ginger
small thumb of root turmeric, or 1 tsp Golden butter (see page 212)
good pinch of black peppercorns
1.5 litres water
1 tbsp apple cider vinegar, or Four thieves vinegar (see page 202)

Roughly chop the carrot, celery or celeriac, onion or leek and garlic. Add to a stock pot with all the remaining stock ingredients apart from the vinegar.

Cover with the water. Bring to the boil, then reduce the heat and simmer gently for 30 minutes. Take off the heat and allow to steep for a further 30 minutes.

Strain, add the vinegar and allow to cool. Pour into a container or use straight away. The stock will keep well in the refrigerator for up to 1 week, or freeze for up to 1 year.

FERMENTED GUT-HEALTH STOCK PASTE

Transform this stock into a dazzling instant soup base by blending all the ingredients apart from the vinegar into a smooth paste. Weigh the paste and add 1g sea salt for every 50g (so if you have 350g of stock paste, you'll need 7g of salt). Find a clean jar that's the right size to cosily house all the ingredients. Pack into the jar and top with an overlapping layer of bay leaves. Scatter a pinch of salt over the bay leaves and fill the jar with enough water to come right to the brim. Seal and ferment at room temperature for 2 weeks, then store in the refrigerator for up to 6 months. To use, spoon 2 tbsp stock paste into a jug and mix with 500ml warm (not boiling) water.

SHOJIN DASHI

Dashi is a seaweed-focused stock that forms the base of nearly all miso soups, as well as other broth-based dishes in Japan. There are many different types of dashi and, often, preserved fish is used to lend umami depth and a little saltiness.

Shojin is a simple vegetarian version which is the easiest to make and the ingredients are pretty widely available. The name refers to *Shojin ryori*, a traditional dining style of Buddhist monks in Japan which dates back to the spread of Zen Buddhism in the 13th century.

As well as being the perfect base for miso or ramen, I also love this in Parsnip toddy and as a base for Kimchi brisket stew (see pages 132 and 143).

MAKES 1 LITRE

2 pieces of kelp
12 dried shiitake mushrooms
4 thin slices of root ginger
1 star anise (optional)
1 tsp tamari, or soy sauce
1 litre water

Place all the ingredients in a saucepan. Simmer gently for a minimum of 30 minutes, or up to 1 hour. You can take it off the heat and allow it to steep further, if you like, for a richer consistency and stronger flavour to the dashi.

Once you have a beautifully infused stock, strain it. I always pluck the shiitake mushrooms out and add them to my soup or other dish. All the other flavourings can be composted or discarded.

BONE BROTH

The trick to a brilliant bone broth is time and apple cider vinegar. Both help draw collagen from the bones. You can either roast the bones first, or use bones left over from cooking any meat. Roasting the bones first results in a darker stock with more depth of flavour; fresh unroasted bones give a lighter stock. Both are brilliant and my decision-making is led by what I've got to hand. If you want a fish bone broth, it's best with unroasted bones, and only use bones from white fish such as hake, sole or plaice (oily fish bones make an unpleasantly greasy broth).

If, like me, you don't eat much meat but want to benefit from bone broths, you can buy jaw-droppingly cheap organic chicken carcasses to make it, giving you the concentrated goodness from the bones. Not only is the jelly-like collagen it produces great for soothing the gut, it's also brilliant for skin – it helps keep it supple, thus slowing the effects of ageing – and eye health, too.

Scale this up or down, making broth any time you have bones small or large. If you only have scraps from a few chicken thighs, harness their goodness by stashing them in the freezer until you have enough to make a batch.

MAKES 1 LITRE

750g–1kg chicken, lamb, beef, pork, game, or fish bones
2 tbsp apple cider vinegar
2 carrots
2 white onions and/or leeks
2 celery sticks, a slice of celeriac and/or a fennel bulb
1 garlic bulb
aromatics, such as garlic, whole chillies, lemongrass, ginger, curry leaves,
    cardamom and/or woody herbs such as bay, rosemary and thyme
2 litres water, or enough to just cover the ingredients

Put the bones and vinegar in a large pot. Let them mingle while you chop the veg (30 minutes is ideal). Roughly chop the carrots and onions (skins on) and/or leeks, the celery, celeriac and/or fennel, into 3–4cm chunks. Halve the garlic bulb. Add the veg with a choice of aromatics to the pot.

Pour in just enough water to cover, then bring to the boil. Reduce the heat and let it gently bubble, lid off, to reduce to a more gelatinous and concentrated broth. The general rule is: the larger the bones, the longer the cook. I give fish bones 30 minutes; chicken 1–2 hours; lamb, beef, pork and game 3–4 hours.

Allow the broth to cool completely with the bones in the pot, as the collagen-drawing continues in the residual heat. For a clearer broth, simply strain; for a richer version, press the contents as you strain. Store for up to 3 days in the refrigerator, or up to 1 year in the freezer.

HERB BROTH

This is the perfect stock to celebrate a glut of woody winter herbs, such as the rosemary, pictured here, which flowers in winter. The broth is a brilliant base for a simple ramen with soba noodles, a boiled egg and foraged greens. It's also a lovely base for blended root veg soups, such as Carrot caraway soup with kefir, or Parsnip toddy (see pages 121 and 132). However, it is equally lovely on its own as a nourishing, restorative bowl of healing hydration.

MAKES 1 LITRE

2 medium onions
1 tbsp olive oil
1 tsp whole black peppercorns
3–4 fresh or dried bay leaves
large handful of any or all of the following: fresh rosemary, thyme, sage, oregano and/or parsley (you can also use dried herbs here)
1 litre water
4 garlic cloves
2 tsp apple cider vinegar
sea salt

Finely slice the onions. Set a large pot over a medium heat. Add the onions, olive oil and a pinch of salt. Stir the onions as they cook to ensure that the oil or onions don't burn, keep the heat at medium-low and let the onions gently cook until glossy and tender. Stir the peppercorns in and let them lap up a little direct heat. Stir in the herbs, again allowing a kiss of warmth to tease out their flavours.

Pour in the water, let it bubble up for a minute and then take off the heat. Peel and grate in the garlic cloves. Allow the infusion to steep like a herbal tea for 15 minutes. Strain, taste and add the vinegar and salt as needed to lift and balance the broth.

Use straight away, or store in the refrigerator for up to 1 week, or freeze for up to 1 year.

DANDELION AND BURDOCK RAMEN

Burdock root has been used since the thirteenth century in holistic medicine, as it's rich in antioxidants and helps remove toxins from the blood. I love it because it has a wonderfully nutty flavour: it's like a root veg version of a water chestnut crossed with banana and hazelnut. Sounds a bit odd, but it's both complex and elegantly simple at the same time.

Burdock and dandelion are both potent liver cleansers, but together the benefits are boosted and naturally promote good digestion, as well as being a powerful tonic for those who suffer from eczema, psoriasis and acne. And, of course, flavour-wise, they are complementary. If you want to go the extra mile, simmer roasted dandelion root (see page 118) or a spoon of chicory coffee with the stock for a rich coffee-like depth of flavour, or keep it simple and add a handful of foraged dandelion leaves. The act of gathering the leaves alone will nourish you (see pages 118–119 for more on foraging).

FOR EACH PERSON

150ml Gut healing veg stock, Bone broth, Herb broth, Shojin dashi, or any stock you love or have to hand (see pages 104, 107, 108 and 106)
100ml fresh-brewed dandelion or chicory coffee (see page 118), or more stock
1–2 tsp miso, soy sauce, tamari, or Black garlic teriyaki (see page 210)
50g dried or fresh noodles (for homemade, see page 116)
a little oil
1 garlic clove
4–5cm piece of burdock root (look in Asian supermarkets)
handful of dandelion leaves

To serve (optional)
thinly sliced spring onion, leek, or chopped three-cornered leek
1 Ramen egg (see page 112), or a simple boiled egg, cooked to your liking
1–2 tbsp pickles
drizzle of sesame oil
toasted sesame seeds

Pour the broth or stock into a saucepan. Set over a low heat and let it start simmering away. Once it's warm, add the dandelion or chicory coffee, if using, or extra stock. Whisk in 1 tsp miso, soy sauce, tamari or black garlic teriyaki to give it richness and body. Taste and add another 1 tsp, if needed.

Cook the noodles separately, according to the packet instructions. Drain them, rinse under cold water, drizzle a drop of oil over, toss it through and set aside. This will keep them from sticking together.

Grate the garlic into the simmering broth and add the noodles. Thinly slice the burdock root. Wash and roughly chop the dandelion greens.

Ladle the soup into a bowl. Add the burdock and dandelion and top with the garnishes of your choice.

MUSHROOM AND EGG RAMEN

A simple, nourishing ramen featuring an iconic ramen egg which is easy and fun to make, but do feel free to swap it out for a straight-up boiled egg, or a vegan alternative such as slices of tempeh, cubes of tofu or additional veg. The mushrooms add body, depth and an immune-boosting boon.

FOR EACH PERSON

250ml Gut healing veg stock, Bone broth, Herb broth, Shojin dashi, or any stock you love or have to hand (see pages 104, 107, 108 and 106)
6g dried mushrooms, or a handful (25g) of fresh mushrooms, thinly sliced
1 Ramen egg (see page 112), or a simple boiled egg, cooked to your liking
1–2 tsp tamari, miso, or Black garlic teriyaki (see page 210), plus more if needed
50g dried or fresh noodles (for homemade, see page 116)
a little oil
1 garlic clove
handful of winter greens
1–2 tbsp pickled veg or kimchi (optional)

To serve (optional)
1–2 spring onions, or ¼ leek, finely sliced
handful of fresh herbs
1–2 tsp sesame seeds, or Mushroom furikake (see page 224)
1–2 tsp chilli oil, or Rayu (see page 194)

Pour the broth or stock into a saucepan. Add the mushrooms. Set over a low heat and let it start simmering away. Prepare the egg, following the instructions on page 112.

Whisk 1 tsp tamari, miso or black garlic teriyaki into the warmed stock to give it richness and body. Taste and add another 1 tsp, if you want.

Cook the noodles separately, according to the packet instructions. Drain them, rinse under cold water, drizzle a drop of oil over, toss it through and set aside. This will keep them from sticking together.

Grate the garlic into the simmering broth. Wash and roughly chop the greens. Add them to the soup along with the noodles.

Ladle the soup into a bowl. Halve the egg and nestle it on the side. Add the pickles or kimchi, if using. Scatter with a selection of garnishes and enjoy. Finishing a bowl of ramen with your choice of extras always feels like a meditation, one resulting in deliciously nourishing edible art.

RAMEN EGGS

The official name for ramen eggs in Japan is *ajitsuke tamago* or *ajitama*. They're basically boiled eggs that are marinated in soy sauce, mirin and sake, though I've suggested a few swaps below to make the recipe as accessible as possible. The idea is that the process adds a sophisticated shaded jacket – bound with umami flavour – to give the egg a starring role in the noodle soup.

If you've ever found peeling boiled eggs a messy faff, try this: add 1 tbsp vinegar (any will do) and a pinch of salt to the boiling water before you put in the eggs. The peel comes off perfectly every time.

Beyond ramen, these eggs are delicious on their own with Mushroom furikake (see page 224), or massage a large handful of kale with a little sesame oil and salt and use it as a salad-y nest for the eggs. They are lovely topped with julienned strips of ginger and chilli oil or Rayu (see page 194).

FOR EACH EGG

1 egg
2 tsp apple cider vinegar, plus a splash more
1 tbsp soy sauce, or tamari
1 tbsp mirin
1 tbsp sake, white wine, or 1 tsp mirin
sea salt

For a soft-boiled egg, bring a pot of water to the boil with a dash of vinegar and a pinch of salt. Ensure your egg is at room temperature and, if not, rinse it under warm water.

Gently lower the egg(s) into the boiling water. For a runny centre, boil for 5 minutes; if you want it a little firmer but still runny, boil for 7 minutes (this is my favourite and most traditional for ramen eggs); for hard-boiled, set your timer for 10 minutes.

Once the time is up, spoon the egg(s) out of the water and rinse under cold water. Let cool slightly, then peel.

Mix up the marinade of soy sauce or tamari, mirin, and sake, wine or mirin in a lidded container, scaling up for any additional eggs. Add the peeled egg(s) to the mix and marinate for at least 30 minutes, or up to 2 days in the refrigerator.

CITRUS MISO

A sunny shade of miso which is brilliant to sip as a nourishing, energy-boosting broth, or to use as a flavour-rich base for a ramen (see pages 110–111) or other soups or stews.

MAKES 1 BOWL

250ml Shojin dashi (see page 106)
1 clementine, or ½ orange
1 tbsp miso
2cm thumb of root ginger
1 small garlic clove
1 spring onion, ¼ leek, or a handful of three-cornered leek
dash of tamari, or soy sauce, to taste
1 tsp seaweed flakes, to serve

Warm the dashi in a saucepan until steaming. While it warms, zest and juice the citrus into a bowl and whisk in the miso.

Cut the ginger into fine julienne strips. Thinly slice or finely grate the garlic. Thinly slice the spring onion or leek, or chop the three-cornered leek.

Whisk the citrus-miso mix into the warm dashi. Add the ginger and garlic. Warm through for 1 minute. Taste and add a little tamari or soy sauce, if needed, to season.

Ladle into a bowl. Top with the spring onion, leek or three-cornered leek and scatter with the seaweed flakes.

Miso

February is the traditional time for making miso in Japan, which coincides with the first signs of blossom, unfurling like a sigh of relief from winter as we gently tiptoe into spring. It's a moment in the Japanese calendar entwined with renewal but also reflection, as the ephemeral beauty of cherry blossom is painted by eloquent haikus, all meditations on the circular pattern of time.

The first time I ever made miso was in February, on my birthday, under the instruction of my friend Yuki Gomi who grew up near Mount Fuji. This was a rare occasion when she was in London at miso-making time, rather than back home with her family in Japan, so we got to emulate the tradition in the cosy confines of her kitchen.

I brought my son along, a reluctant ten-year-old back then, and we spent the day together sipping tea as a cauldron of organic soy beans steamed in the pressure cooker. Once tender and slightly cooled, we collectively sprinkled in salt and *koji*, fungi-inoculated rice: the magic ingredient which transforms the cooked beans into deeply flavoured, nourishing, umami-rich paste.

What I loved most about the experience was the wait. While you can speed up the process by using less salt and thus create a faster-maturing paste with less depth, a traditional jar of miso should be tucked away for a full year before opening. So I waited.

On the morning of my next birthday, I retrieved a step ladder to help me reach the jar I'd tucked away in a cool, dark cupboard in my bedroom. The contents had been transformed from a thick, lumpy jumble with flecks of *koji* into a silky smooth, dark mahogany paste. The smell was like an autumn breeze in a woodland near the sea, with faint hints of melting chocolate and delicate wafts of dried porcini.

Opening the jar not only stirred the senses, but also memories of the year that had been and gone, and those in my life who'd arrived or drifted away within the four seasons that had passed.

SIMPLE HOMEMADE SOBA NOODLES

I'm an enormous fan of buckwheat flour. While I'm not coeliac or gluten free, I know lots of people who can't tolerate wheat and the western diet is certainly far too reliant on the grain as a staple crop. Ancient varieties of wheat used to be perennial, growing much more slowly, which offered the opportunity for more nutrients to be lapped up from the soil as the plant's roots dug deeper and became more resilient.

What's brilliant about buckwheat is that it has lots of positive nutritional and soil-regenerative properties. Buckwheat is often used as a 'green manure', to nourish soil in between crops. In terms of health, buckwheat is one the best plants for protein: like quinoa, it contains the nine amino acids that make up a complete protein.

Buckwheat soba noodles are also woven into Japanese winter traditions, as they are the traditional dish of choice eaten on New Year's Eve in most areas of Japan. The tradition started around the Edo period (1603–1867) and there is a widespread belief that long soba noodles symbolise a long life. Buckwheat is also a hardy crop, surviving severe weather, which has led to soba noodles being seen as a symbol of strength and resilience.

MAKES ENOUGH FOR
4 BOWLS OF SOUP

250g buckwheat flour, plus extra to dust
1 tbsp psyllium husk powder, or xanthan gum
½ tsp sea salt, or 1 tsp fine nori flakes
150–200ml warm water, plus more if needed
1–2 tbsp olive oil, or flaxseed oil

Mix the flour, psyllium husk or xanthan gum and salt in a large bowl. Add the water, little by little, stirring it in as you go, until it comes together into a soft, workable dough a bit like soft modelling clay in texture.

Knead the dough for a minute or 2 to help the psyllium husk or xanthan gum absorb all the water, adding a little more water if the dough gets dry or crumbly as you knead. Once kneaded, drizzle 1 tbsp of the oil over and work it into the dough, adding a little more if needed.

Generously dust a large clean work surface with buckwheat flour. Cut the dough into 4 pieces: each should be roughly the size of a clementine and will give you enough noodles for a decent-sized bowl of ramen. The dough freezes well (use it within 6 months), or store in the refrigerator, wrapped in a beeswax wrap or greaseproof paper, for up to 3 days.

Roll the dough out as thinly as you can, as thin as a paperback book cover, if possible. If you have a spatula or dough scraper, it's useful to help keep the dough from sticking to the work surface. I use it to help lift and unstick the dough, adding a little flour as I gently ease the dough up.

You should end up with a thin sheet of dough roughly the size of an A4 sheet of paper (albeit one with wonky, rounded edges). You can trim the edges if you like, or just have some noodles that are shorter. Use a large knife to cut the dough into thin noodles (I like mine 5mm thick and 7–8cm long, give or take).

You can cook them straight away, but they benefit from drying at room temperature for half an hour before cooking if you can wait. You can leave them longer, too, if you like: up to 12 hours (covered with a cloth) at room temperature.

To cook, simply add to simmering stock and cook for 2–3 minutes or until tender right the way through.

Wild winter wonders

Brave the cold and venture outside for a dander to gather a few wild things for your dinner. I never regret it when I do – even if it takes me quite some time to bundle up enough motivation, especially on a grey day – because inhaling a lungful of fresh air and spending a moment connecting with nature is one of the best winter remedies. And it becomes one you can eat, if you harness the ancient wisdom of foraging.

FORAGING TIPS

Never take more than one-third of what you find. You want to ensure that there is plenty left to regenerate, as well as enough for wildlife to feast on.

Always wash foraged finds and try not to pick them from places where dogs pee, or where local councils might spray. This is particularly relevant for town and city parks and the green parts of council estates: if you ever see a patch of yellow grass, it's probably because the council are spraying to kill the weeds you fancy foraging! So always be careful, know the land you're harvesting from and ensure that you are certain you know what you're collecting.

BAY LEAVES   I'm convinced that I've never been more than a few metres away from a bay tree! They're wildly prolific throughout Europe and beyond, planted ornamentally for their handsome stature and sprays of fragrant evergreen leaves. Bay is brilliant for calming the nerves. The aromas released from pinching a few leaves on a branch are nearly as soothing as the act of consumption.

CLEAVERS   This is a plant that wants to be known. Even if you don't recognise it by name, it's likely that a walk through any grassy field or hedgerow-lined path has left your clothing decorated with little burrs or sticky weeds. 'Goosegrass' and 'sticky Willie' are two other monikers given to this thin, hairy, green-leaved grass, with its small rosettes along the vertical stem and tiny, four-petalled white flowers as the weather warms up. The young tips are great in salads or in Wild and sprouted falafel (see page 64). Eating them helps support your lymphatic system, notably the glands around your throat that become sore and swollen when you have a cold or flu.

CONIFERS   Like bay leaves, conifers are evergreens, which means they offer a rich plumage of green forage throughout the year. The name alludes to the trees' most defining characteristic: they produce cones. While pines are the most prominent cone-bearing conifers, firs and spruce also fall into this category. This means you can technically eat your Christmas tree (but make sure it hasn't been treated with chemicals). One conifer that certainly is not edible is the poisonous yew, so take care when foraging and try to go with experts to help you navigate what is and isn't safe (and see the list on page 278). Once you've got that knowledge at hand, you can open up a world of free, nutrient-rich foods. Pine is good in a cough remedy tea (see page 276), but also provides a wonderfully lemongrass-like back note to all manner of dishes, such as prasorizo or meatballs (see pages 162 and 176) and it's lovely added to broths.

DANDELION LEAVES AND ROOTS   The elegant, serrated leaves of the nutritionally mighty dandelion are easy to find throughout the year, typically lining garden paths or growing along walls. A handful of leaves added to salad, used in Wild and sprouted falafel or added to a smoothie (see pages 64 and 46) will give your liver some love; our livers help our bodies get rid of toxins, so they always appreciate foods that help them out. I dig up dandelion roots, scrub them clean, cut into 2cm pieces and roast until they turn from creamy white to a deep shade of chocolate. Ground to a powder, this smells and tastes like instant coffee and can be used the same way.

GORSE FLOWERS   As the weather gets colder, the hedges around where I live start to turn golden. A rather invasive shrub, gorse is beautiful (if prickly) and the densely packed yellow petals house a surprisingly exotic coconut scent, which reminds me of a sun cream I used as a teenager. Such warming thoughts are just what I want in winter, but I also love the tropical taste of the flowers. My favourite way of using them is to steep them in a basic kombucha (see page 290), but they're also lovely added to salads or used as a garnish for Chocolate, pear and miso mousse (see page 260).

MAHONIA FLOWERS   I always associate yellow flowers with the arrival of spring, though daffodils are not edible, and forsythia is safe to eat but doesn't taste of much.

Mahonia, however, is a yellow flower heralding the start of winter. It always cheers me up, as it does the bees, who dive in for a final winter forage before closing up shop. The holly-like leaves are a prickly obstacle, but surpassing them to gather a handful of flowers is worth it for their tongue-tingling lemon sherbet tang. Use in salads, or as a garnish for Carrot caraway soup with kefir or Roasted squash mousse (see pages 121 and 264).

PENNYWORT   I think pennywort looks like nasturtium leaves: rounded, with a soft scalloped edge and a stem that offers a belly button-like dot in the centre of each leaf. They grow at the base of oak trees or along hedgerow banks. You find them throughout the year, but I always notice them most in winter when little else is about. They have a succulent-type texture, juicy with a jelly-like centre to each leaf, which can be gut-soothing. The leaves are also antibacterial. Eating them – they're lovely in salads – can help the body to fight infection.

ROSEHIPS   I always think rosehips look like the fictional glowing nose of the most famous reindeer of all. In the winter, a mass of thorny wild dog rose stems can look like a tangle of matte red Christmas lights. I like rosehips best after the first frost, when they become soft enough to squeeze out their pulp like toothpaste. The hips, once picked, can be crushed, steeped in water and strained to make a vitamin C-rich tea or syrup, which you can sweeten with honey. I love the syrup drizzled over Kefir labneh with roasted rhubarb (see pages 256 and 238).

ROSEMARY BLOSSOM   Another evergreen, rosemary looks a bit like a conifer, but it's actually related to sage. Rosemary's name comes from the Latin *ros marinus*, or 'dew of the sea'. I've foraged native coastal rosemary in Australia and it has a wonderful saltiness, but cultivated rosemary is more like pine in flavour. I often see it in the wild and, in winter, it produces tiny orchid-like flowers in a delicate shade of violet. They're sweet at first bite, with a robustly herbaceous finish. I love using them to finish Celeriac Seville ceviche (see page 74).

SEA BEET   Most plants edging the coast will lap up the salty flavour of the sea and wild beetroot is a delicious example. The thick green leaves are more succulent than garden-grown beetroot leaves, but look very similar; the main difference is that the wild sort grows in tighter clusters and you can't see the roots peeping out from the soil. They are also usually fully green, with no pink veins. They're rich in iron and delicious cooked as greens, or use small tender leaves in salads.

SEAWEED   While spring is the main season for seaweed foraging, fresh growths of greens flourish on the seabed year round. The key is to go out at low tide and gather seaweed that is still rooted in the soil. Take scissors, as you don't want to uproot the plants or you'll deprive yourself, others and marine life of food for the future. Seaweeds to seek include dulse (*Palmaria palmata*), a deliciously rich source of vitamin C, kelp (*Laminaria digitata*), which you can use fresh or dried to make dashi (see page 106), and protein-rich carrageen (*Chondrus crispus*). You need to be cautious of a seaweed called *Desmarestia*, as it's high in sulphuric acid, though as it grows in deep water, it is unlikely you'll come across it.

SLOES   The small, plummy fruits emerge in autumn but often hang around into winter. I preserve them in a salt brine (100ml water mixed with 4g sea salt: scale up as needed) with a few bay leaves and black peppercorns. After 4–6 weeks, they're transformed into something akin to an olive, with a wonderfully plummy back note.

THREE-CORNERED LEEK   The precursor to wild garlic, typically emerging early in the new year. It looks like a grassy version of spring onion greens and tastes similar.

VIOLETS   Unmistakable tiny purple flowers that grow in the shade, typically along woodland paths, violets have a delicately sweet perfume that matches their taste. The leaves are edible, too, and a great addition to winter salads. They typically emerge in late February.

WOOD SORREL   Like the shield-shaped leaves of common sorrel, wood sorrel has the same lip-smacking lemony sourness but it looks completely different: like a smaller version of clover that's often a rich bronze colour with tiny yellow flowers. I always see it on the edges of groups of other plants. It acts as a weed encroaching on a row of winter lettuces, or I've often had it take over the pot of a dormant patio plant. It also grows in parks along shadier walls or fences.

CARROT CARAWAY SOUP WITH KEFIR

This is a stunner of a soup I made to refuel and rehydrate after running a half marathon. I intentionally made too many roast carrots the day before, so I'd have leftovers to repurpose the next day.

I've popped my favourite method for cooking carrots below, gleaned from Heston Blumenthal. A similar recipe is in his book *Family Food*, which is packed with brilliant cooking techniques.

If you're dairy free, an almond milk-based kefir, or coconut kefir, is a brilliant alternative and a good flavour pairing with the caraway. I also love this recipe with cardamom and/or pink peppercorns in place of the caraway.

SERVES 4

500g carrots
4 garlic cloves
2 tsp caraway seeds
1 bunch of thyme
2 tbsp olive oil
2 tbsp unsalted butter, or coconut oil
500ml veg stock, Gut healing veg stock, or Herb broth (see pages 104 and 108)
250g kefir (see recipe introduction), plus more to serve
sea salt and freshly ground black pepper

To serve (optional)
three-cornered leek, or rosemary flowers
linseed oil, pumpkin seed oil, or blackcurrant seed oil

Cut the carrots diagonally into 1cm-thick slices. Peel the garlic and lightly crush with the side of a kitchen knife. Toast the caraway seeds in a hot, dry pan for a few minutes, until they release their aroma. Meanwhile, tie the thyme with kitchen string so it's easy to retrieve after cooking.

Place the carrots in a pan large enough to accommodate them in a shallow layer, add the garlic, caraway, thyme, olive oil and butter or coconut oil. Set over a low heat. Cover and cook for an hour or so, until the carrots are done. Check the pan every 10 minutes or so, as the idea is for the carrots to cook in the moisture created by the butter and the vapour in the pan.

Once the carrots are cooked, remove the lid and increase the heat. Continue to cook, turning regularly, until lightly browned on all sides. Spoon into a blender with half the stock. Start blending, feeding in more stock, until the soup is smooth and creamy and as thick or thin as you like it. Pour into a saucepan to gently heat through, swirling in the kefir just before serving.

Season as needed and serve warm with an added swirl of kefir, three-cornered leek or herb flowers and a few dots of oil, if you like.

INSTANT ENERGISING GREEN SOUP

Made like a savoury smoothie, then warmed like a soup, this is the easiest green soup you can make and a perfect antidote to the winter blues.

FOR EACH PERSON

75g winter greens, such as kale, spinach, watercress and/or coriander
75g sprouted (see page 66) or cooked white beans, or chickpeas
1 garlic clove, peeled
1 tsp Winter five spice (see page 230), or ground cumin, or to taste
1 tsp Preserved citrus paste (see page 198), or 1 tsp finely grated lemon zest and 2 tbsp juice, or to taste
250ml stock, or water
hint of vinegar, to taste (optional)
sea salt and freshly ground black pepper

To serve (optional)
Digestive dukkah (see page 226)
flaxseed oil, or olive oil
microgreens

Bring a pot of water or a kettle to the boil. Roughly chop the greens, removing any woody stems. Place in a heatproof colander and rinse well. Once the water is boiling, pour it over the greens until they are tender, glossy and bright. Rinse under cold water. Pat dry and bundle into a blender or food processor.

Add the sprouted or cooked beans or chickpeas, the garlic, spice, preserved or fresh citrus and stock or water. Blend until smooth.

Pour into a saucepan. Taste and adjust the spicing and seasoning and vinegar or lemony tang, as needed. Gently warm through.

Delicious with a finishing sprinkling of Digestive dukkah, a drizzle of flaxseed oil or olive oil and/or microgreens.

KAPUŚNIAK

Perogies stuffed with potato and sauerkraut are one of my favourite comfort foods and this Polish classic is a like a soup version of them! I add the sauerkraut right at the end, after cooking, to retain all its magnificent properties. When fermented, the vitamin C content of cabbage is up to 50 per cent more than that of raw cabbage, and it's easier to digest as all the complex starches and sugars have been broken down. Its sour note is lactic acid – created by the bacteria as they work their magic – and the flavour it brings here is the perfect complement to the hearty winter veg.

SERVES 4

2 carrots
2 parsnips
2 leeks and/or onions
1 tsp caraway seeds
1 tsp juniper berries (optional), ground
½ tsp ground allspice, or a pinch of mixed spice
1 tbsp olive oil
1 litre stock, Bone broth, or Gut healing veg stock (see pages 107 and 104)
2 boiled potatoes
2 garlic cloves
400g sauerkraut (for homemade, see page 72)
sea salt and freshly ground black pepper
handful of fresh green herbs and/or rye sourdough crumbs, or shreds of leftover beef, chicken or lamb, to serve

Finely chop the carrots, parsnips and leeks and/or onions. Set a large pot over a medium heat. Add the chopped veg, caraway seeds, juniper, if using, and allspice or mixed spice along with a good pinch of salt and pepper, the olive oil and a splash of the stock. (The stock means you don't use as much oil and you also avoid getting the oil to smoking point, which can destroy its benefits and flavour.)

Gently cook the veg until softened and caramelised, 5–10 minutes. Add the remaining stock, increase the heat a little and let it bubble away as you finely chop the potatoes and finely chop or grate the garlic.

Add the potatoes and garlic to the bubbling broth. Let them warm in the broth for 5–10 minutes, until hot and tender. Take the soup off the heat. Fold the sauerkraut through, adding enough of its brine to taste.

Ladle into bowls and finish with fresh green herbs and/or rye sourdough crumbs, or shreds of leftover beef, chicken or lamb.

MEDICINAL CHINESE CHICKEN SOUP

Soups are a pivotal element of Chinese cuisine. They're valued for their flavour, of course, but also for their ability to soothe the digestive system and prevent or cure illness. Chinese soups in winter are tailored with herbs to help boost the body's warmth and energy and to help support the lungs, which are more susceptible to ailments in winter as cold, dry air can irritate airways and cause coughing, wheezing and shortness of breath. This soup is crafted to nourish and protect you and it also tastes heavenly: soothing, comforting and a classic example of the magic power of chicken soup.

One element that's relatively easy to source for this soup is goji berries. Also known as Chinese wolfberries or 'happy' berries, these tangy fruits are used by herbalists to help eyesight, protect the liver, boost immune function and promote longevity.

Red dates or jujubes are also a brilliant addition, if you can find them. These dense dates can calm the nervous system, protect the liver and moisten the lungs, which will help with the bronchial issues that tend to creep up on us in the winter.

If you don't eat meat, you can swap the chicken for 500g mushrooms and 500g aromatic stock veg, such as carrots, fennel, celery, celeriac and parsnip, or – for a simpler bowlful – add some Chinese herbs to Gut healing veg stock (see pages 127 and 104).

SERVES 4–6, WITH LEFTOVER CHICKEN FOR ANOTHER DISH

selection of Chinese herbs (see page 127, use all of them if you like, with 10g of each)
500g–1kg chicken on the bone (you can use a whole chicken, jointed pieces such as legs, wings or thighs, or chicken carcasses)
2 leeks and/or onions
thumb of root ginger, sliced into 1cm pieces
2 tbsp goji berries
4 jujubes (red dates), or 4 prunes
1–2 heads of pak choi, cut into wedges, or ½ green or white cabbage, finely shredded
sea salt, soy sauce, or tamari, to season

To serve
raw carrot ribbons
julienned root ginger
handful of fresh herbs

Soak any Chinese herbs you wish to use in a large bowl with enough water to just cover. You don't want them swimming in liquid, but 50–75ml for every 10g herbs should be enough to hydrate the herbs and give some deliciously flavoured liquid to add to the soup. Set aside for 30 minutes.

Place the chicken in a pot large enough to hold it fully (if it's peeping out of the top a bit, that's ok: you can slide the pot into a 160°C/150°C fan oven if it is, to help ensure even cooking).

Quarter the leeks (halving both horizontally and vertically), then clean well, and/or quarter the onions. Add them to the pot with the ginger, goji berries, jujubes (red dates) or prunes along with the Chinese herbs and their soaking liquid.

Pour over enough water to cover the chicken or come most of the way up the pot: you need to leave 3cm or thereabouts headroom to accommodate the broth bubbling, to ensure it doesn't boil over.

Place the pot over a medium-high heat initially, to bring the water up to a gentle boil. Once it's bubbling away, reduce the heat to medium-low and simmer gently, basting the top of the chicken if it's peeping out from the broth. Alternatively, cook in the centre of the oven, basting the top with the broth every 30 minutes or so. Cook for 1½ hours. Take off the heat and let it rest for a further 30 minutes, then remove the chicken to a platter. Strain the broth from the solids. Pluck out the goji berries, if using, and return to the broth.

Many Cantonese people consume the broth without the meat, but you can shred the chicken and fold it into the broth with wedges of pak choi or shredded cabbage. Season with salt, soy sauce or tamari. Simmer to warm everything through before serving.

Spoon the soup into bowls and garnish with ribbons of carrots, julienned strips of ginger and/or a handful of fresh herbs such as coriander or thyme.

Chinese herbs for winter

Employ the wisdom of Chinese medicine with traditional herbs to give you more vitality in the cold months. You can use all the herbs below in Medicinal Chinese chicken soup (see page 124) in the suggested quantities, or cherry-pick from the list, trying just a couple. You can easily source the following herbs online (I've listed my favourite suppliers in the Directory, see page 302).

ASTRAGALUS ROOT (*huáng qí*)   Valued as an immune-boosting tonic. It's also very nourishing for the kidneys.
Add 5 pieces or 10g to the soup.

CODONOPSIS ROOT (*dǎng shēn*)   A stress-relieving root. It helps with adrenal fatigue caused by stress, lack of sleep or too much work, can combat tiredness – thus giving you an energy boost – and help with digestive problems, too.
Add 5 pieces or 10g to the soup.

CHINESE WILD YAM (*shān yao*)   This root benefits the spleen, lungs and kidneys. It can boost energy and alleviate bodily weakness.
Add 3 pieces or 10g to the soup.

ANGELICA SINENSIS (*dāng guī*)   This is a warming herb that nourishes the blood and invigorates blood circulation. It has a long history in traditional Chinese medicine for women's health, helping throughout different stages from menstruation pain to childbirth recovery to menopause.
Add 3 pieces or 10g to the soup.

SOLOMON'S SEAL (*yù zhú*)   These golden slivers of curly herb are believed to treat ailments related to the lungs and throat, alleviating dry coughs, sore throats and thirst.
Add 3 pieces or 10g to the soup.

ESHKENEH: PERSIAN PENICILLIN

This is an ancient recipe that dates back to the Parthian Empire, which was strategically situated on The Silk Road as a major political and trade power from 247 BC to 224 AD, stretching from what is now central-eastern Turkey to eastern Iran. It's the humblest of soups and easy to construct. While fenugreek leaves, dried or fresh, are a staple ingredient, you can swap them for fresh herbs or greens and, if you have some ground fenugreek to hand, add it for flavour and its anti-inflammatory properties.

SERVES 4

4 onions
2 garlic cloves
1 large handful of fresh fenugreek leaves, or 4 tbsp dried fenugreek leaves
2 potatoes, or ¼ celeriac
2 tbsp olive oil
4 fresh bay leaves
1 tsp ground turmeric, or a thumb of root turmeric, finely grated
1.5 litres vegetable stock, or chicken stock, or Gut healing veg stock
    (see page 104)
2 tbsp verjus, or apple cider vinegar, or Four thieves vinegar
    (see page 202), or to taste
2 tbsp lemon juice, or to taste
2 eggs
sea salt and freshly ground black pepper

Halve the onions, peel and finely slice. Finely chop the garlic. Finely chop the fenugreek leaves, if using fresh. Chop up the potatoes into little cubes – unpeeled for maximum nutrients – or peel and chop the celeriac (the peel is too woody to leave on).

Set a saucepan over a medium heat and add the oil and onions. Gently cook the onions until just tender, 5–10 minutes. Add the garlic and gently cook until just softened, about 30 seconds.

Add the bay leaves and turmeric and fold through to give a kiss of heat before adding the cubed potatoes or celeriac and fenugreek leaves, fresh or dried. Stir through. Pour in the stock and increase the heat, then bring to the boil. Reduce the heat to low, cover and cook for 15 minutes until the potatoes or celeriac have cooked through. Add the verjus or vinegar and the lemon juice, stir and taste. Add a touch of salt if needed.

Lightly beat the eggs in a small bowl and add 4 tbsp of the broth from the soup to help temper the eggs, then pour into the soup. Simmer for 5 minutes, stirring. Season with lots of pepper and more verjus, vinegar and/or lemon juice, as needed. Spoon into bowls and eat straight away.

SPANISH SWEET POTATO SOUP

I love the simplicity of this soup, as well as the lazy approach! I often tumble wedges of squash or whole sweet potatoes into the oven and then think about how to use them later, as I know they'll form the base of a delicious meal. What's brilliant about this recipe is there's a lot of raw goodness. The oil isn't heated. You could lightly toast the spices if you like, but I find the purity of untoasted alluring here. You also have raw garlic, which lends a layer of spice, but its inclusion is subtle and softened by the velvety sweetness of the sweet potato. Leaving the skin on the sweet potato offers more body, depth and fibre. Once blended, you'd never know it was there.

SERVES 4

2 sweet potatoes, or 500g squash
1 litre chicken stock, veg stock, or Gut healing veg stock (see page 104)
1 tbsp fennel seeds
1 tbsp cumin seeds
1 tbsp coriander seeds
good pinch of saffron threads, or 1 tbsp smoked paprika
2 garlic cloves, peeled
2–4 tbsp olive oil, plus more (optional) to serve
finely grated zest and juice of 1 lime, or 1 tbsp sherry vinegar, or apple cider vinegar
sea salt and freshly ground black pepper

To serve (optional)
Digestive dukkah (see page 226)
microgreens (see pages 94–95), or thyme leaves

Preheat the oven to 200°C/190°C fan. Wash the sweet potatoes, pierce all over and slide into the oven to roast for 45 minutes or until fully tender right the way through: the skin should be crinkly and collapsed a little. If using squash, cut into 4–5cm wedges and roast, skin on, until meltingly tender. Warm the stock over a medium heat until steamy.

Remove the sweet potatoes or squash from the oven. Place them in a blender, skins and all, with the spices, garlic, 2 tbsp olive oil and half the warmed stock. Start blending, whizzing in more stock and oil as needed until it is as thick, creamy and rich, or as thin, as you like.

Season with a generous grinding of pepper, lime zest and juice or vinegar to lend acidic balance, and enough salt to tickle your taste buds.

Delicious finished with a drizzle of olive oil and a light dusting of Digestive dukkah and microgreens or thyme leaves.

PARSNIP TODDY

Ginger, lemon and honey are great flavour companions for sweet parsnips and this velvety winter soup is just what you need to knock a cold on its head. To nudge the soup further into hot toddy territory, you could add a snifter of whisky, another excellent flavour match for this earthy root.

SERVES 4

2 white onions, peeled, or 4 leeks, white and pale green parts only
2 tbsp olive oil, or butter
4 parsnips, peeled and finely sliced
3 garlic cloves, peeled and chopped
about 1 litre chicken or vegetable stock, Shojin dashi, Herb broth, or Bone broth (see pages 106, 108 and 107)
thumb of root ginger, finely grated, or to taste, plus julienned root ginger (optional) to serve
finely grated zest and juice of 1 lemon, plus more zest (optional) to serve
leaves from 3 rosemary sprigs, finely chopped
2 tbsp honey, or to taste, plus more (optional) to serve
sea salt and freshly ground black pepper

To serve (optional)
drop of whisky
small rosemary leaves or flowers

Finely chop the onions or leeks. Place a large pan over a medium heat. Once hot, add the oil or butter, then the onions or leeks with a pinch each of salt and pepper. Reduce the heat and cook, stirring often, for 5 minutes or until tender and lightly golden.

Add the parsnips and chopped garlic, stir through and cook for a minute or so, then pour in the stock. Simmer gently for about 20 minutes until the parsnips are mashably tender.

Add the ginger, lemon zest and juice and the chopped rosemary, along with 1 tbsp of the honey. Blend until lusciously smooth, adding a little water, if needed, to thin the soup. Taste and add salt and pepper and more honey, if needed. Adjust the spicing too, if needed, adding a little extra ginger if you like.

Divide the soup between bowls. It is lovely finished with a few julienned strips of ginger and finely grated lemon zest, a ripple of honey, a few dots of whisky and rosemary leaves or flowers.

LEMON-BARLEY AVGOLEMONO

Lemon barley water is an old-fashioned tonic that dates to ancient Egypt. Along the Egyptian coast, people imbibed a fermented drink called *kashkab*, made with barley, citron leaf, mint, rue and black pepper. This is said to be the origin of lemonade as we know it today, as well as the more health-focused lemon barley water.

I've woven the nutritious pairing – which is great for helping your kidneys flush out toxins – into a Greek classic which is also known as a cure-all: *avgolemono*. It's the ultimate comfort soup: the barley is nutty, nourishing and soothing, while the lemon adds an invigorating zing. When mixed with the egg, the broth acquires a luxurious creaminess. It's one of my all-time favourite soups.

SERVES 4

4 leeks, white and pale green parts only, or 2 white onions
1 litre chicken stock, veg stock, Gut healing veg stock, or Bone broth
  (see pages 104 and 107)
200g sprouted barley (see page 66), or cooked barley
2 egg yolks, or 1 whole egg
finely grated zest and juice of 2 lemons, plus more juice if needed
4 garlic cloves
200g watercress, kale and/or purple-sprouting broccoli
sea salt and freshly ground black pepper
extra-virgin olive oil, or linseed oil, to serve

Finely slice the leeks or onions, ensuring you rinse all the grit from the leeks. Combine the stock, leeks or onions and barley in a large saucepan. Season with salt and pepper. Bring to the boil, then reduce the heat and simmer for 10 minutes to soften the leeks or onions and barley.

In a heatproof bowl, whisk the egg with most of the zest from the lemons and 100ml of the lemon juice. Slowly add 4 tbsp hot stock to the egg mixture, whisking constantly. Remove the soup from the heat, then slowly stir the egg mixture back into the broth. Return it to the heat. Peel and finely chop or grate the garlic. Stir it in with the greens, saving a few small green leaves back to serve, then cook to gently soften the greens and garlic.

Taste and season with salt, pepper and more lemon juice, as needed. Ladle the soup into bowls. Garnish with the remaining greens, lemon zest and a drizzle of olive oil or linseed oil.

FERMENTED CELEBRATION BARSHCH

Winter is a great time to be fermenting, as it brings new energy to stored veg at a time of year when fresh food is scarce. This soup is built around traditional Polish *kvass*, a ferment made with rye bread, beetroot and water. It is based on a Christmas eve barshch recipe from a 1952 book by Maria Disslowa: *Continental European Cooking*. The book has a foreword by Dr Wit Tarnawski, director of a well-known health resort in the Carpathian mountains, in which he highlights the importance of cooking from scratch. 'Home cooking cannot be neglected nor passed over with indifference, if one sincerely desires health for one's self and one's family.' You can also try this infused with dried or fresh hawthorn berries, to boost heart-healthy properties as well as flavour.

SERVES 4

For the *kvass*
250g raw beetroot
30g piece of rye bread (about 2 tbsp when chopped)
1 tbsp dried or fresh hawthorn berries (optional)
500ml water

For the soup
1 litre chicken, fish or veg stock
2 star anise and/or juniper berries (optional)
4 bay leaves
250g celeriac, or parsnip
1 onion
25g dried mushrooms, or 120g fresh mushrooms
1 garlic clove
sprinkle of dill and/or pine needle powder
sea salt and freshly ground black pepper

Chop the beetroot and the bread. Place in a 1.5–2 litre jar with the hawthorn berries, if using, and cover with the measured water. Stir, cover with a cloth and ferment at room temperature for 3–4 days.

Strain the *kvass*, reserving the liquid, and discard or compost the bread. Rinse the beetroot and finely chop it.

Bring the stock and star anise and/or juniper and bay to the boil. Finely chop the celeriac or parsnip as well as the onion. Add the beetroot, celeriac or parsnip, onion and mushrooms to the boiling stock. Reduce the heat to a simmer and cook until the vegetables are tender, about 20 minutes. Remove the star anise and/or juniper.

Take off the heat, then grate in the garlic and add the *kvass* liquid. Finely chop the dill, if using. Taste and season well with salt and pepper, add the sprinkling of dill and/or pine needle powder, then serve.

RASAM WITH CAULI POPCORN

Rasam is a classic example of traditional functional food, as all the ingredients have clear nutritional benefits. The tamarind-enriched tomato soup has South Indian origins and is favoured in Ayurvedic medicine for its cold-fighting properties.

If you have a pot of Winter five spice (see page 230), use it here, swapping out the cumin, black pepper and cinnamon for the same amount (1 tbsp plus 2 tsp) for even more depth and warming complexity.

SERVES 4

1 onion
3 tbsp ghee (for homemade, see page 214), or coconut oil
1 tbsp ground cumin, plus more (optional) for the cauliflower
1 tsp freshly ground black pepper
1 tsp ground cinnamon
1 tsp black mustard seeds
10 curry leaves
300g soaked or sprouted (see page 66) split red lentils
400g tomato passata, or 200g tomato purée plus 200ml more stock or broth
500ml veg stock, Bone broth, or Gut healing veg stock (see pages 107 and 104), plus more if needed
1 cauliflower
grating of nutmeg or a pinch of garam masala (optional)
2 garlic cloves
2 tbsp tamarind paste
sea salt and freshly ground black pepper

Set a large pot over a medium heat. Halve, peel and finely slice the onion. Melt 1 tbsp of the ghee or coconut oil with the onion and a pinch of salt. Reduce the heat and gently cook for 5–10 minutes until tender and glossy.

Fold in the spices, curry leaves, lentils, passata, or tomato purée mixed with its 200ml stock or broth. Stir well. If using passata, let it reduce a little, then pour in the 500ml stock. Pop a lid on and simmer for 30 minutes, checking occasionally to ensure there's plenty of stock (top up with more stock or water, if needed: it should be like a soupy dal).

Preheat the oven to 200°C/190°C fan. Set a large roasting tray on the top shelf to heat up.

Trim the leaves and hearty, creamy stem from the cauliflower, leaving you with just the florets: these will become crispy roasted, crouton-like 'popcorn'. Strip a handful of soft greens from the cauliflower. Give them a good wash, pat dry and finely shred. Set aside. Use the remaining cauliflower heart and leaves to make a kraut or kimchi (see pages 72 and 206).

Put the remaining 2 tbsp ghee or coconut oil in the warmed roasting tray. Add the cauliflower florets with a good pinch of salt and pepper. Stir through the ghee or oil and roast for 15 minutes or until the florets are a little crispy and coloured around the edges. Once cooked, remove from the oven and grate over a good dusting of nutmeg or garam masala, if using, or swap for another spice such as cumin.

Once the lentils are tender, grate in the garlic and stir through. Take off the heat. Add the tamarind, little by little, tasting as you do; I like mine quite sour, but you might want to use less than the full 2 tbsp if your taste buds say otherwise. Adjust the seasoning and spicing to your liking and loosen with a little water if needed.

Spoon into bowls and top with the roasted cauliflower florets and shredded cauliflower greens.

PERUVIAN CORIANDER STEW

Although coriander leaves are tender and delicate, they thrive in cooler climates and grow happily under a bit of cover in the winter alongside all the spicy Asian salad greens such as mizuna and mustard. In this stew, the herb takes centre stage, its citrusy herbaceous notes are complemented with the zest and juice of lime: a classic Peruvian pairing. It makes a stunningly bright and fragrant bowlful.

While this stew is fish-inspired, if you don't eat fish – or if the weather is unkind to your local fishermen – you can easily swap treats of the sea for nuggets of parboiled potatoes. Try to get your hands on the nutty, nutrient-dense small purple or red varieties such as Purple Peruvian or Chiquilla Pitiquiña, or have a go at sourcing *oca*, one of the oldest Andean crops, a sweet and tangy tuber with sunset shades, even if you do include fish. These ancient potatoes are slower-growing, richer in flavour and a taste of the diversity that heritage vegetables bring. In Peru, there are more than 4,000 varieties of potato.

SERVES 4

1 onion
1 tbsp coconut oil
1 tbsp coriander seeds, or 2 tsp ground coriander
2 tsp ground cumin
2 tsp ground cardamom
60g coriander (you can top up with microgreens, see page 94, or other soft green herbs such as fennel, basil, mint and/or parsley)
4 garlic cloves
2–3 limes
400ml coconut milk, or water
500ml fish stock (for homemade, see page 107), or veg stock
200g parsnip, potato and/or celeriac
500g winter white fish and/or shellfish (or add additional potatoes and/or winter veg, see recipe introduction)
large handful (50–100g) of winter greens
sea salt and freshly ground black pepper

Set a large pot over a medium heat. Halve, peel and finely slice the onion. Put the onion and coconut oil in the pot with a pinch of salt. Reduce the heat and gently cook until the onion is glossy and tender. Swirl in the coriander seeds, cumin and cardamom. Take off the heat and let it cool for a moment.

Bring a kettle to the boil. Set the coriander and any other herbs into a sieve. Pour the boiling water over, then immediately rinse under cold water: this will give the broth a bright green colour. Pat dry, chop and spoon into a blender or food processor with the spiced onions, garlic cloves, finely grated zest and juice of 2 limes and coconut milk or water. Blend to a smooth paste.

$\longrightarrow$

Pour the stock into the pot you used for the onions. Bring to the boil. Finely chop the parsnip, potato and/or celeriac. Add the veg – along with any extra you are using if replacing the fish and shellfish – and simmer in the broth until tender.

Cut the fish into large bite-sized pieces (about 5cm) or clean if using shellfish (debeard any mussels, see page 169, cockles or clams, or clean veins from prawns or langoustines). Add the fish and cook for 5–10 minutes until warmed and cooked through.

Add the coriander paste and cook a minute or 2 longer, until it has lapped up a steamy swirl of heat. Fold in the greens and let them collapse into the heat of the stew. Taste and add more lime zest and/ or juice, salt, pepper or any additional seasoning or spice tweaks.

Serve warm. This is best served on the day of making, but if you chill it quickly and fully warm it back through, you can refrigerate it for up to 2 days, or freeze for up to 6 months.

KIMCHI BRISKET STEW

Inspired by a dish called *yukgaejang*, that pairs the warming spice of kimchi with slow-cooked beef. Classic recipes don't use full-on kimchi (just gochujang), but adding the fermented cabbage at the end – so you get the benefits of the live ferment – gives the dish a vitamin C boost. It also lends an extra portion of veg which marries beautifully with the beef.

SERVES 4–6

500g beef brisket, stewing steak, or chopped beef
1 onion
1–2 tbsp ghee (for homemade, see page 214), or coconut oil, plus more
  if needed
1 tbsp Chinese five spice, or 2 star anise (optional)
2 tbsp soy sauce, or tamari
4 garlic cloves
4 slices of root ginger
8 dried shiitake, 10g dried mushrooms, or 1 tsp mushroom powder
4 bay leaves and/or a bundle of fresh thyme, tied with kitchen string
1.5 litres freshly boiled water
400g kimchi
sea salt and freshly ground black pepper

To serve (optional)
4 spring onions, or a handful of three-cornered leek, sliced or chopped
large handful of sprouted mung beans, or microgreens (see pages 66 and 94)
1 tbsp sesame oil
1 tbsp lightly toasted sesame seeds

If using brisket or stewing steak, cut along the grain into 6cm pieces. Halve, peel and finely slice the onion. Set a large pot over a medium heat. Add the ghee or oil and the meat. Cook for 5–10 minutes, or until it starts to brown.

Add the onion to the pan and cook for a moment longer, so it softens and colours a little, adding more ghee or oil, as needed. Add the Chinese five spice or star anise and soy sauce or tamari and sizzle for 1 minute.

Bash the garlic cloves and remove their skins. Add them along with the ginger slices and mushrooms or mushroom powder and herbs. Pour over the freshly boiled water. Bring to the boil, then reduce the heat and simmer away for 1½–2 hours or until the meat is fall-apart tender.

Fold the kimchi through: if it is chunky, give it a rough chop first. Taste and adjust the seasoning as needed.

Spoon into bowls. This is delicious as is, but lovely with spring onions or three-cornered leek, sprouted mung beans or microherbs, a drizzle of sesame oil and a scatter of sesame seeds.

WARMING

MAIN

COURSES

Electricity, especially during the winter,
sparks us into a false sense of night and day.

I read a fascinating article about a couple in Manhattan who lived off grid. In such a wired city – one that never sleeps – it's a remarkable feat. But they wanted to reconnect with natural patterns.

In winter, dinner time was directed by the early setting Sun. Candlelight fed post-prandial reading, followed by bed. Their days shortened in winter. Their eyes closed with the fading sunlight just like a flower that closes at night but opens at sunrise and, by noon, is completely unfolded. This phenomenon is called *zeitgeber*, which is an environmental cue to our natural daily rhythms. The Greek philosopher Theophrastus observed it in his seminal studies of plants, likening their behaviour to human instincts.

COMFORT IS KEY

While humans aren't inclined to go into full-on hibernation like dormice or hedgehogs, our bodies do crave more rest when days are shorter. I've crafted the recipes that follow with this in mind. Comfort is key, not just in a soul-warming, taste bud-pleasing sense, but also in terms of digestion. While everyone's body responds differently to the elements – be they light or foodstuffs – the intention is to create dishes that soothe the body and set the scene for a cosy night of rest. With that in mind, I've aimed to make the dishes as light on prep, and washing-up after, as possible.

We've evolved to go against the grain, but some people suffer in their toil against the rhythms of nature.

CARROT MISO MAC

Mac n cheese is the ultimate comfort food at any time of year. In winter, it hits an even sweeter spot. This veg-boosted twist offers the same look and texture, to my mind, as boxes of Kraft did when I was a child growing up in America. We ate a lot of amazing homegrown food cooked from scratch, but there were also plenty of packets and boxes such as Hamburger Helper and crinkly foil-wrapped parcels of bone-dry waves of ramen noodles with their tiny sachets of salty seasoning. This mac dishes out a rich lick of nostalgia, but, to go with it, there's a delicious dose of immune-boosting nutrients, too.

SERVES 4

4 carrots (total weight about 500g)
200g cashews
water, chicken stock, or Gut healing veg stock (see page 104), to cover
300g wholegrain macaroni, or gluten-free elbow macaroni, or
    600g previously cooked and cooled pasta (see page 154)
1 tbsp olive oil
2 tbsp miso, or to taste
1 tbsp Dijon mustard, or to taste
2 garlic cloves, peeled
pinch of cayenne pepper, or chilli powder (optional)
sea salt and freshly ground black pepper

To serve (optional)
4 tbsp breadcrumbs, or crushed cashews
smattering of herbs, such as coriander, a mix of microgreens
    (see page 94), or thyme

Cut the carrots into 1cm (or thinner) slices. Tumble into a saucepan with a pinch of salt and the cashews. Pour in enough water or stock to just cover. Bring to the boil, reduce the heat, pop a lid on and simmer for 15–20 minutes or until the carrots are fully tender.

Cook the pasta according to the packet instructions. If using cooked and cooled pasta, simply refresh it in a pot of boiling water and drain after 1 minute, or as soon as it has warmed through. Toss with the oil.

Blend the carrots, cashews and their liquid with the miso, mustard and garlic. Taste, season and add more miso and/or mustard and a pinch of cayenne pepper or chilli powder, if needed.

Fold the carrot sauce through the cooked and drained pasta. I love serving this in a baking dish topped with breadcrumbs or crushed cashews and grilled until brown, then scattering over a fresh pop of herbaceous greenery.

COCONUT CREAMED KALE ALOO

I make this all the time as a base for what's known as 'ripped chips' at River Cottage, the organic smallholding in Devon where I teach fermentation and seasonal nutrition. The 'ripped' part is a nod to the preparation. You boil the potatoes first, then let them cool fully; this also transforms the way your body takes in the starch, turning the potatoes from fast-burning fuel into slower, more sustainable energy that feeds the good bacteria in your gut (see page 154). Once cooked, you then literally rip – or lightly crush then tear – the potatoes into bite-sized pieces. When the cold potatoes hit the hot oil, they turn marvellously crisp. It's such an indulgent, comforting dish that gives you sleep-easy, end-of-the-day fuel. I love it.

SERVES 4

For the spiced roast potatoes
1kg floury potatoes, such as Maris Piper or King Edward
3–4 tbsp coconut oil
2 tbsp coriander seeds, fennel seeds and/or cumin seeds
1 tsp curry powder, or Winter five spice (see page 230, optional)
sea salt and freshly ground black pepper

For the coconut creamed kale
400g kale
4 garlic cloves, finely grated
thumb of root ginger, finely grated
thumb of root turmeric, finely grated, or 1 tsp ground turmeric
400ml coconut milk

Bring a large pot of salted water to the boil. Give the potatoes a scrub clean, then plunge them into the water whole. Boil until tender right the way through (but not falling apart), about 30 minutes, depending on size.

Drain the potatoes. Allow to cool fully, then rip them into bite-sized pieces (about 2cm nuggets). You could cut them with a knife, but ripping them gives them rougher edges that crisp beautifully when cooked. Leave the skins on: they'll become crisp and add texture as well as nutrients.

Preheat the oven to 220°C/210°C fan. Set a large roasting tin on the top shelf to heat up.

Put 3 tbsp coconut oil in the roasting tin and slide it into the oven for a minute to heat up. Season the potatoes with salt and pepper. Remove the tin with the hot oil from the oven and carefully fold the ripped potatoes through the oil. Roast for 25 minutes until golden and crisp, turning them a couple of times during cooking and adding more oil, if needed.

While the potatoes cook, make the kale. Bring a pot of salted water to the boil. Strip the kale leaves from their woody stalks (use the stalks to make a relish, see page 196, juice or smoothie).

Plunge the kale into the boiling water, then drain immediately and run under cold water. Squeeze dry, roughly chop and put in a bowl or blender. Add the garlic, ginger, turmeric and coconut milk. Blend to a creamed spinach-like consistency. Season to taste and gently warm.

Fold the coriander, fennel or cumin seeds and curry powder or Winter five spice through the potatoes as soon as they're cooked. Spoon the warm creamed kale into a bowl, or on to a serving dish, then top with the roast potatoes, along with their oil and any spices left in the pan.

Carbs left to go cold

Pasta, potatoes and rice are all carbohydrates that cause a surge in blood glucose levels as they are broken down. For people with diabetes, these surges in glucose can be tricky to manage and cause problems over time. Simply changing the way you prepare and cook these starchy foods can transform the way your body absorbs them.

Starch is essentially a chain of glucose molecules linked together. Glucose from cooked starchy foods – such as white rice, pasta and potatoes – is absorbed almost as quickly as glucose from a sugary drink.

However, when starchy foods are cooled, their structure is reorganised once more and the digestive enzymes in your gut can't break them down as easily. This is a good thing, as it allows their starch to travel through the gut to reach the microbes in the colon, providing them with just the sort of food they like (prebiotics).

Eating freshly cooked potatoes, pasta and rice causes the biggest rise in blood glucose.

Eating chilled potatoes, pasta and rice causes a slightly lower rise.

Potatoes, pasta and rice that are cooked, quickly chilled, then reheated fully, cause the lowest rise of all.

Thus, a little advance prep (make a batch of rice, pasta or potatoes the night before you want to eat them) both saves time and gives your health a boost.

Dairy in winter

It's easy to forget that cheese essentially emerges from the landscape, with grass being essential to its production. Like fruits and vegetables, it is affected by the seasons. Mass manufacturing gives us cheese year-round, but this affects the flavour, texture and nuances which make artisan cheese so enjoyable.

On a traditional dairy farm, everything slows down in winter. November to March is a restful period, until warmer spring rains come and turn the pastures green. As fresh blades of grass emerge, heifers bring new life. The new mothers produce most of their milk after calving and the lush summer pastures provide rich nutrients which are recycled into the milk. As the growing season wanes, preparation for winter takes place. Grass is cut and dried as hay, or fermented as silage, which helps retain its nutrients. As temperatures drop, the cows' milk production slows. Many traditional cheeses are only made with summer milk, and are then aged to enjoy during the colder months.

If you've ever noticed that fresh dairy tastes funny in winter (my son does), this is typically due to the fermented funkiness from silage. The colour is also different, as fresh grass provides beta-carotene (the same substance that lends carrots their hue) that gives butter a golden summer glow. Of course, beta-carotene also gives us a health boost.

Not only does eating aged cheeses in winter give you a preserved taste of summer, but the ageing process also involves fermentation. This helps break down the natural sugars or lactose in the cheese which is often the (literal) hiccup for some people when it comes to consuming dairy, as it can be hard to digest.

AGED CHEESES TO TRY IN WINTER

Mont d'Or, Stilton, extra mature (18 month+) artisan Cheddars (Montgomery, Westcombe, Keen's), Chevrotin des Aravis, Comté, Époisses, Gruyère.

ROOTY RUMBLEDETHUMPS

A classic winter comfort food from the Scottish borders, very similar to Ireland's colcannon or England's bubble and squeak. Potato often features in place of – or alongside – the root veg, but my version leans more toward roots and, for me, they win out over the spuds. They're also easier to digest, which will help with a more restful slumber. If you're vegan, try using oat milk in place of dairy and swap out the cheese for breadcrumbs mixed with garlic and a little olive oil: it's equally indulgent.

SERVES 4

1kg root veg (parsnips, swede, turnips and/or celeriac)
4 garlic cloves, crushed
1 tbsp butter, olive oil, or coconut oil, plus more for the cabbage or kale and onion or leek
½ green cabbage, or 3 large handfuls of kale (total weight 200g)
1 onion, or leek, finely chopped
150g Cheddar cheese, or similar cheese
leaves from a couple of thyme sprigs
sea salt and freshly ground black pepper

Peel the root veg and cut it into 2–3cm chunks. Tumble them into a large pot and cover with water. Add a good pinch of salt, a good twist of pepper and the garlic.

Bring to the boil, then cook until the spuds and roots are mashably tender, about 30 minutes. Drain, then mash or purée with the butter or oil and season to taste.

Preheat the oven to 200°C/190°C fan.

Set a large frying pan over a medium-high heat. Cut the cabbage or kale into thin shreds (by all means use the kale stalks, but ensure you thinly slice them). Add the cabbage or kale and onion or leek to the pan and sizzle them in a little butter or oil until tender and glossy. Season well. Remove the pan from the heat while the cabbage or kale is still bright green, then stir it through the mash.

Bundle the cabbage/mash medley into a baking dish. Grate the cheese and scatter it over the veg. Bake until the cheese is golden, about 25 minutes. Scatter with thyme leaves and serve.

CAULIFLOWER 'LASAGNE'

This dish is a rich celebration of winter cheese, aged to provide us with a cold-weather food that gained its flavour and nutrients from summer grass. To make it wildly indulgent, without compromising the digestive system (or a good night's rest), I've swapped the classic lasagne's meat and pasta for caramelised layers of roast cauliflower. Think lasagne-meets-cauliflower cheese: two winter comforts bundled into one. Even if you're not sure about cauliflower, this might just win you over.

SERVES 4–6

2 cauliflowers
3 tbsp ghee (for homemade, see page 214), butter, or olive oil
1 onion, or leek, finely chopped
1 tsp fennel seeds
2 tbsp fresh thyme leaves and/or rosemary leaves
100g fresh mushrooms, or 25g dried mushrooms such as porcini, rehydrated
2 × 400g cans of tomatoes
250ml stock, or Gut healing veg stock, or Bone broth (see pages 104 and 107)
125ml red wine, or white wine
4 garlic cloves
200g aged melting cheese, such as Cheddar, Gruyère, Comté, provolone, black truffle Fontina, or, even better, *caciocavallo*, grated
sea salt and freshly ground black pepper

Preheat the oven to 200°C/190°C fan. Place a large baking tray on the top shelf. Cut the base and leaves off the cauliflowers (save the greens for a side dish). Cut the white heads of the cauliflowers into 1–2cm slices. The centre parts will give large 'steaks'; the sides will crumble a little, but use it all.

Drizzle 2 tbsp ghee, butter or olive oil over the hot baking tray. Arrange the cauliflower slices in as shallow a layer as possible, seasoning as you go. Roast for 25 minutes or until just tender and with caramelised golden edges (they will finish cooking in the sauce, but you want them fairly tender first).

Set a large pan over a medium-high heat. Add the remaining ghee, butter or oil with the finely chopped veg and a good pinch of salt. Reduce the heat and cook until tender and just golden. Fold in the fennel seeds, thyme and mushrooms and cook down until the mushrooms are tender. Add the tomatoes, stock and wine. Let it bubble up over a medium heat and reduce by half, about 20 minutes. Grate the garlic cloves as it cooks (see page 160) and fold them through right at the end.

Layer the cauliflower and sauce in a large baking dish, about 27 × 21cm, or 25cm in diameter. Scatter the cheese over and bake for 30 minutes until bubbling and golden (crank the heat up, or turn the grill on, if it needs a nudge). Let rest for 5 minutes before serving with a salad or greens.

MUSHROOM MUJADDARA

Mujaddara is from Mesopotamia, in modern-day Iraq, and the oldest recipe dates from 1226. It pairs lentils with rice; the grain and pulse together offer the perfect package of amino acids to make a complete protein. It's a staple of Arab Christians during Lent, when meat is avoided, and is so highly revered that it led to the saying, 'A hungry man would sell his soul for a dish of mujaddara.' In Palestine, rice is replaced with bulgur, a delicious swap. I use sprouted lentils and rice (see page 66). It makes it easier to digest and faster to make. If you don't have time for a full sprouting, soak the lentils for 30 minutes in water and 1 tbsp apple cider vinegar, then rinse and cook.

SERVES 4

400g sprouted green, coral, or black lentils (see page 66), or 200g dry lentils (see recipe introduction)
200g wild or brown basmati rice, or bulgur wheat, or 300g sprouted wild or brown basmati rice, or bulgur wheat (see page 66)
3 tbsp ghee (for homemade, see page 214), coconut oil, or olive oil
1 tbsp cumin seeds, or 2 tsp ground cumin
1 litre stock or broth
50g dried mushrooms (porcini are amazing here), or 200g fresh mushrooms
2 onions, finely sliced
2 garlic cloves
handful of herbs, fresh or dried (I love rosemary, sage, thyme and lavender)
splash of balsamic vinegar (optional)
1 lemon
sea salt and freshly ground black pepper

Set a large pot over a medium heat. Put in the lentils, rice or bulgur, 1 tbsp of ghee or oil and the cumin. Cook for 1 minute, then add the stock and the mushrooms, if dried. Simmer for 45 minutes, until the stock is absorbed.

If using fresh mushrooms, finely slice them. Set a large frying pan over a medium-high heat. Add the mushrooms with a pinch of salt but no oil. Cook for 5–10 minutes, stirring, to help cook out the water, which will intensify the flavour. Once they start to look dry, fold in 1 tbsp ghee or oil and cook until nicely coloured. Add a good hit of pepper and more salt.

Preheat the oven to 200°C/190°C fan with a large roasting tray on the top shelf. Add the remaining ghee or oil to the tray. Fold the sliced onions through with a generous pinch of salt. Arrange so the onions are spread out and not overlapping: the idea is to crisp them up to add texture and crunch. Roast for 15–20 minutes, stirring halfway, so the outer onions don't burn.

Once the lentils and rice are tender and the stock absorbed, grate in the garlic. Stir in with the herbs, balsamic, if using, the finely grated zest of the lemon and a squeeze of its juice. Serve with the crispy onions on top.

BROCCOLI BRAVAS

Most of broccoli's benefits are reaped when eaten raw, but if you chop the broccoli (or any of its brassica relatives: Brussels sprouts, kale, cabbages or cauliflower) first and then wait 40 minutes, it produces its most powerful antioxidant: sulforaphane. If you cut and cook broccoli straight away, that doesn't have time to develop, so getting organised in advance means you get more from every bite. A similar rule applies to garlic: chop or crush it and set aside for 10 minutes before using. During this time, allicin, which helps prevent certain cancers, is created and stays intact during cooking (see page 302).

SERVES 2 AS A MAIN COURSE,
OR 4 AS A SIDE DISH

2 heads of broccoli, or 400g purple-sprouting broccoli
2–3 tbsp oil, or ghee (for homemade, see page 214)
1 onion, finely chopped
4 garlic cloves, finely chopped
1 tsp chopped fresh thyme leaves, or rosemary leaves
1 tbsp smoked paprika
1 tbsp ground cumin
200g tomato purée
250ml Gut healing veg stock (see page 104), or water
400g cooked chickpeas or beans, or sprouted chickpeas (see page 66)
1–2 tbsp apple cider vinegar, or sherry vinegar
sea salt and freshly ground black pepper

To serve (optional)
finely grated lemon, lime or orange zest, plus a little juice
handful of soft green herbs (parsley, coriander, three-cornered leek),
    finely chopped
4 tbsp almonds (crushed Marcona or toasted flaked almonds are brilliant),
    or a handful of toasted breadcrumbs

Trim 2–3cm off the base of the broccoli. Quarter the florets if larger, or halve if smaller. If using purple-sprouting broccoli, just trim any woody ends and cut larger pieces to marry in size with the smaller. Set aside.

Set a large frying pan over a medium heat with the oil or ghee. Add the onion with a pinch of salt, reduce the heat and gently cook for 10–15 minutes until golden and meltingly tender. Fold in the garlic, thyme and spices. Cook gently for a minute to soften before adding the tomato purée, stock and chickpeas or beans. Let it simmer away for 15 minutes or until the stock has reduced down and the sauce is rich and thickened. Stir through the vinegar and season with salt and pepper to taste.

Bring a pot of salted water to the boil. Preheat the oven to 200°C/190°C fan. Plunge the broccoli into the boiling water. Drain straight away, though save the water for your plants! (The nutrients from the broccoli will do them good.) Shake or pat the broccoli dry.

Arrange the sauce in a baking dish, or keep it in the frying pan if it's ovenproof and large enough for the broccoli, too. Nestle the broccoli on top of the sauce and slide into the oven. Bake for 20 minutes or until the broccoli is tender right the way through.

Finish the broccoli with a grating of citrus zest, a squeeze of juice, a smattering of chopped herbs and a dusting of crushed almonds, or toasted breadcrumbs, if you like. This is delicious on its own, or with a simple side dish of rice or roasted sweet potatoes and salad.

WINTER LEEK PRASORIZO

In the winter, leeks are a valuable staple. Prasorizo is almost poetic in its simplicity, an elegant Greek rice dish featuring little other than sweet winter leeks, new season's olive oil, lemon and herbs. Use dried herbs if you haven't got fresh, or snip in some fresh pine needles for a citrusy, complementary flavour. The nutmeg is not traditional, but a delicious suggestion from my son Rory. The spice is soporific, making it a great help towards the dream of a restful evening slumber.

SERVES 4

3 large leeks, or 6 smaller leeks
6 tbsp new season's olive oil, plus more (optional) to serve
2 tbsp thyme and/or rosemary leaves, fresh or dried, plus more to serve
2 garlic cloves
200g raw risotto rice, or 400g cooked and chilled risotto rice
   (see page 154)
200–400ml Gut healing veg stock, Herb broth (see pages 104 and 108),
   or water, plus more if needed
1 lemon
generous grating of nutmeg
sea salt and freshly ground black pepper

Finely chop the leeks, right the way down to the dark green ends: they have the most goodness and will soften into tender strands once cooked. Place in a colander and rinse under warm water to ensure they're fully cleaned and to help soften them in the warmth of the water. Shake dry.

Set a large pot over a medium heat. Add the cleaned leeks with all the olive oil and a good pinch of salt and pepper. Gently cook for 10 minutes to further soften the leeks.

Add the herbs to the leeks. Peel and grate in the garlic cloves. Add the rice. If using raw rice, pour in 400ml stock or water, or use just 200ml if you're using cold cooked rice. Stir the stock or water through and pop a lid on. Simmer on the hob for 20 minutes if using raw rice or 10 minutes if the rice is already cooked. Stir halfway through to ensure it doesn't catch on the bottom and add more stock or water, if needed.

Take off the heat and let it sit, lid on, for a further 5 minutes. Remove the lid. Finely grate in the zest of the lemon. Season with salt, pepper and a good squeeze of lemon juice as well as a generous grating of nutmeg. Add a finishing gloss of olive oil, if you like, and an extra smattering of herbs, then serve.

CELERIAC TACOS WITH KIMCHI AND SMOKED MACKEREL (OR MUSHROOMS)

The celeriac swap for corn tortillas – trust me, it's not a gimmick, the humble root truly makes a phenomenal canvas for all your filling flavour – means you can happily double the amount of tacos you normally eat, as the base is so light, yet deeply rich in flavour. It's the perfect way to indulge in a diversity of foods, which is one of the key pieces of advice for maintaining a healthy microbiome, the epicentre of human health. As well as a happy tummy, you'll have tap-dancing taste buds, as these tacos are out of this world. The key to a great taco is to layer in the flavours, but don't overfill it.

SERVES 4

For the taco shells
1 celeriac
1 tbsp olive oil
sea salt and freshly ground black pepper

For my favourite taco fillings
100g houmous, or Mayan pepita pesto (see page 218)
250g smoked mackerel, or L'escargot mushrooms (see page 86)
250g kimchi (for homemade, see page 206)
100g watercress, soft winter leaves, or microgreens (see page 94)
4 tbsp red onion slices, or Mexican taco pickles (see page 188)
4 tbsp toasted seeds, or Digestive dukkah (see page 226)

Preheat the oven to 180°C/170°C fan.

Carve the skin from the celeriac using a knife (veg peelers don't always stand up to the tough skin). The ends of the celeriac are likely to be too small to make a decent-sized taco shell, so cut a slice from the smaller end to expose a circular area similar to a corn tortilla-like shape.

Using a large sharp knife, cut it into slices as thin as possible. A medium celeriac should yield around 12 tortilla-like rounds (cut more if needed). Some slices have little cracks in them, from the celeriac splitting during growth. You can use offcuts to patch it up: trim the offcuts so they're not too large or thick, just big enough to fully patch the cracked area. A sprinkle of salt helps the patches stick.

Line a large baking tray with greaseproof paper. Drizzle a little olive over (about 1 tsp) and dust with a pinch of salt and pepper. Baste each slice of celeriac in the seasoned oil on both sides and arrange in a single layer. You'll probably get 4–6 slices on the paper. Top with another layer of greaseproof paper and continue to layer up the remaining celeriac slices, giving each layer a light basting of oil and some seasoning. Cover the top layer with greaseproof paper and set a dish or another baking tray on top to keep the celeriac slices flat. Slide into the centre of the oven and bake for 15 minutes: this softens the celeriac in readiness to quickly sear before serving.

Meanwhile, get all the toppings ready. You can either have bowls on the tables for DIY assembly, or layer up the fillings before serving.

To sear the taco shells, set a large frying pan over a medium-high heat, simply add 1–2 baked celeriac rounds to the pan (no oil needed) and cook for 1–2 minutes, or until lightly golden and charred on each side (return them to the oven to keep warm while you sear the remaining shells).

A delicious filling assembly is a layer of the houmous or Mayan pepita pesto, topped with smoked mackerel or cooked mushrooms, followed by kimchi, soft greens, raw or pickled red onions and a dusting of seeds.

TEN-MINUTE MUSSELS
WITH A TRIO OF SAUCY OPTIONS

Rope-grown mussels are about as ecologically friendly as aquaculture (seafood farming) gets. The process is sheer minimalism. There are no inputs: no chemicals or feed are required to keep the mussels healthy or make them grow. There is no need for captive breeding as the young seed mussels, called spat, are collected by hanging hairy ropes in the sea during spawning season: the wild juvenile mussels simply attach themselves to the ropes.

The mussels are microscopic when they first settle on the ropes, but within a year to fifteen months, in fertile waters, mussels can grow to be full of sweet, kelpy-flavoured orange meat, ready to make a delicious healthy meal full of vitamins, minerals and omega-3 oils. Best of all, they take all the nutrients they need simply by filtering the sea water that ebbs and flows around them.

Mussel farms can also provide a positive ecological benefit to the waters in which they are sited. The mussel-clad ropes make a weedy underwater jungle that attracts other sea life, too. The farm becomes a habitat and nursery for all kinds of creatures, including anemones, starfish, marine worms, crabs, lobsters and many types of fish.

Rope-grown mussels are a winter treat and, even better, they're one of the fastest feasts you can make. Below and overleaf are three saucy ideas for the shellfish. I can't ever decide which to have and often prep a bowl of each sauce, then simply divide the steaming, just-cooked-and-opened mussels straight into them. Just warm the bowls of sauce in a low oven as you cook the mussels, then serve them on the table with some slabs of bread, oil or butter and a big salad.

Each sauce is enough for 1kg mussels, or 4 servings as a main course

MISO COCONUT

400ml can of coconut milk
1 tbsp miso, or to taste
1 leek, or 4 spring onions, finely sliced, or a handful of three-cornered leek, finely chopped
freshly ground black pepper

Whisk the coconut milk and miso together in a heatproof bowl or saucepan. Taste and add a little more miso, if you like. If you're using leek, place it in a colander and pour over boiling water to soften it and ensure that all the grit gets cleaned out. Add the leek, spring onions or three-cornered leek to the miso coconut base and season with a good hit of pepper.

Gently warm over a medium heat if using a saucepan, or place the heatproof bowl in an oven preheated to 180°C/170°C fan to warm through as you cook the mussels (it'll only take 5 minutes to warm up). The freshly steamed mussels will warm it further.

NEAPOLITAN

200g tomato passata
200ml veg stock, or Gut healing veg stock (see page 104)
1 garlic clove, finely grated or chopped
1 tsp dried oregano or basil, or 2 tsp chopped fresh oregano or
    basil leaves
sea salt and freshly ground black pepper

Whisk the passata and stock together in a heatproof bowl or saucepan.
Add the garlic along with the herbs and season with salt and pepper.

Gently warm over a medium heat if using a saucepan, or place the
heatproof bowl in an oven preheated to 180°C/170°C fan to warm
through as you cook the mussels (it'll only take 5 minutes to warm up).
The freshly steamed mussels will warm it further.

TOMATO GINGER

200g tomato passata
200ml veg stock, or Gut healing veg stock (see page 104)
2 tsp miso
1 leek, or 4 spring onions, finely sliced, or a handful of three-cornered
    leek, chopped
small thumb (3–4cm) of root ginger
freshly ground black pepper

Whisk the passata, stock and miso together in a heatproof bowl or
saucepan. If you're using leek, place it in a colander and pour over
boiling water to soften it and to ensure that all the grit gets cleaned
out. Add the leek, spring onions or three-cornered leek to the tomato
miso base. Cut the ginger into thin julienne strips, or finely grate it,
then add to the sauce. Season with a good hit of pepper.

Gently warm over a medium heat if using a saucepan, or place the
heatproof bowl in an oven preheated to 180°C/170°C fan to warm
through as you cook the mussels (it'll only take 5 minutes to warm up).
The freshly steamed mussels will warm it further.

Mussels demystified

BUYING AND STORING MUSSELS

Mussels are meant to be living when you buy them, so they need oxygen to stay alive and be safe to eat. They should smell briny, like the sea. If they smell bad, don't buy them! Equally, don't buy mussels if their shells are cracked.

The shells should be tightly closed. If a shell is open, give it a firm tap on the work surface. If it closes, it means it's still alive and safe to eat. If it doesn't close, discard it.

They're best eaten the same day as they are bought, but can happily be stored for 24 hours in the refrigerator. As soon as you get them home, place in a colander, rinse under cold water and set the colander over a large bowl. Cover with a cloth and put it in the refrigerator.

HOW TO CLEAN MUSSELS

Clean the mussels right before you cook them. Working with one mussel at a time, rinse the shell under cool running water and scrub it gently to remove any debris. If there is something that looks like some hair, this is the 'beard': it's a bit of the rope that they were grown on and should be removed before cooking. To de-beard the mussels, grab the beard and pull it towards the tail (narrow) end of the mussel. Most of the time it will come out with a firm tug. If not, you can cut it with a pair of scissors as close to the shell as possible.

HOW TO COOK MUSSELS

Find a large pot with a tight-fitting lid. Pour in 2–3 tbsp of water, just enough to steam up and tease the mussel shells open. Too much will dilute the broth.

Bring the liquid to a rapid boil, add the mussels all at once and clamp the lid on the pot. Set a timer for 3 minutes. When the timer goes off, gently stir the mussels and push any that have not opened to the bottom of the pot (being closer to the heat will help them to open).

Let the mussels cook for 2 minutes more (5 minutes in total), then remove the pot from the heat and discard any shells that have not opened. Spoon into a bowl of one of the sauces (see pages 166 and 168) and eat straight away.

If you have any leftover mussels, you can eat them cold the next day if you store them in the refrigerator, but never reheat cooked mussels.

MONTHS WITH AN 'R'

September marks the traditional start of the shellfish season, as the seas start to cool around this time, ending the hot summer spawning period. Hence the tradition of eating shellfish in months than contain an 'R'. Reducing consumption in the warmer months (May to August) allows them time to repopulate, giving us plenty to feast on during the winter.

BRITISH BRODETTI FISH PIE

Along the Adriatic coast, fisherman celebrate a share of their catch by making the simplest of fish stews while still at sea, using the few condiments available on board. In the fishing port of Fano in Italy's Marche region, the humble fish stew is called *brodetto di pesce*, then as you travel the coastline there are subtle riffs on the dish's name and its contents. But that's where the true joy of cooking lies: a delicious recipe is often a celebration of what is available and at its best at any given time, and in winter it's especially important to embrace the sweetest gifts from the sea on offer. Ultimately, *brodetto* is a classic case of a dish that came into being as a way of making a virtue of necessity. It has been likened to a jazz standard, a theme open to infinite variations, and that's the reason why – albeit following a guiding thread – no two *brodetti* are alike. The recipe here – though made with local fish – has the classic brodetti flavours of fennel and capers, wine and tomatoes.

The Italian Renaissance chef Bartolomeo Scappi wrote in his monumental cookbook, *Opera dell'arte del cucinare*, 'I believe fishermen are abler with fish than cooks, because they cook it as soon as they catch it.' Brodetti is simplicity itself and I've left the canvas minimal here, but one embellishment I have made is to add potatoes. The stew is normally an elegant assembly of just the freshest fish in a stock-and-wine-enriched tomato base. I've housed it under a layering of olive oil-kissed potatoes, which crisp up a little and protect the fish as it gently cooks under the potato crust. It's a lovely twist on the classic British creamy mash-capped fish pie.

SERVES 4–6

500g potatoes
3 tbsp olive oil
1 small fennel bulb, 2 celery sticks, or a 2–3cm slice of celeriac,
    finely chopped
1 onion, finely chopped
1 tbsp fennel seeds
150ml dry white wine
400g can of crushed tomatoes
1 tsp white wine vinegar
400ml stock (bought fish stock, or fish Bone broth, see page 107,
    gives depth and the ultimate kiss of the sea, or see tip, overleaf)
4 garlic cloves, finely chopped or grated
500g white fish fillets, cut into 5cm pieces (or see tip, overleaf)
1 tbsp capers (optional)
2 tbsp fresh thyme leaves
1 lemon
sea salt and freshly ground black pepper

Bring a large pot of salted water to the boil. Give the potatoes a scrub clean. Plunge them into the water whole. Boil until tender right the way through, but not falling apart, about 30 minutes, depending on size. Set aside while you make the fish stew.

Set a large saucepan over a medium heat. Add 1 tbsp of the oil along with the fennel, celery or celeriac and onion, adding a pinch of salt. Fold in the fennel seeds, reduce the heat and gently cook for 10 minutes, or until tender and glossy.

Increase the heat to medium-high, add the wine and simmer for 5 minutes, or until half-reduced. Add the tomatoes, vinegar and stock and cook over a medium-high heat for 20 minutes until well flavoured. Fold half the garlic through the sauce. Taste and season with salt and pepper, as needed.

Preheat the oven to 200°C/190°C fan.

Spoon half the sauce into a baking dish (something with a width or diameter around 20cm). Arrange the fish on top evenly. Scatter with the capers and half the thyme, then spoon on the remaining sauce. Season with a light dusting of salt and a generous amount of black pepper.

Finely slice the cooked potatoes. Season with salt, pepper, the finely grated zest of the lemon, a squeeze of lemon juice and the remaining thyme and garlic. Coat them in the remaining olive oil. Create a lightly overlapping layer of the potatoes over the fish stew, fully covering it, but not overlapping the potatoes too much.

Slide into the oven on the top shelf and cook for 30 minutes or until the potatoes are nicely golden. The fish will cook beautifully and perfectly in this time. Let it rest for 5 minutes before serving. Delicious with a big wintry salad, or a side of steamed seasonal greens.

NOSE-TO-TAIL FISH VERSION

If you're up for buying whole fish to fillet yourself, 1kg should offer 500g flesh, plus enough bones to make Bone broth (see page 107). Just make sure the fish has had its gills removed, and wash out any blood line from the inside, which may make the stock bitter. (Or just ask your fishmonger for bones; they often give you those for free.)

PERSIAN POMEGRANATE POULET

On the longest night of the year, this Persian pomegranate and walnut stew, called *fesanjan*, helps keep the darkness at bay. The winter solstice marks both the darkest part of winter and the return of the light. If you are part of the Iranian diaspora, that celebration is Shab-e Yalda, which stretches into the morning hours. The festivities mark the light winning over darkness. This dish is symbolic of health and vitality and thus often plays a starring role on the Shab-e Yalda table.

SERVES 4

1–1.5kg jointed chicken pieces (legs, thighs, drumsticks and/or wings)
2 onions, finely sliced
1 tbsp olive oil
4 garlic cloves, finely chopped
1 tsp ground turmeric, or a thumb of root turmeric, finely grated and/or a generous pinch of saffron threads
1 tsp ground cumin
½ tsp ground cinnamon
½ tsp freshly grated nutmeg
½ tsp freshly ground black pepper
4 bay leaves
finely grated zest and juice of 1 orange
200ml pomegranate molasses
250ml Gut healing veg stock, or Herb broth (see pages 104 and 108)
1 tbsp honey (optional)
100g walnuts
sea salt
smattering of coriander, thyme leaves and/or microgreens (see page 94), to serve

Preheat the oven to 200°C/190°C fan. Set a large baking dish in the oven.

Season the skin of the chicken with a pinch of salt. Once the baking dish is hot, add the chicken, skin side down. Nestle the onions around, drizzle the olive oil over and slide into the oven on the top shelf. Roast for 15 minutes. The onions will start to soften and caramelise in the melting chicken fat.

Add the garlic with all the spices, bay, orange zest and juice. Pour over the pomegranate molasses and stock. Return to the oven for 45 minutes.

Remove the chicken from the oven. Taste the sauce and drizzle a little honey over to balance the sweet with the sour pomegranate molasses, if needed.

Place the walnuts on a baking tray with a pinch of salt and slide into the oven to lightly toast for 5–10 minutes. Crush or chop the walnuts and scatter over the chicken, along with the herbs. Serve warm with a big salad, or a side dish of greens such as Turkish tahini greens (see page 92).

ODE TO SWEDISH MEATBALLS

Sweden's King Charles XII is one of the most fascinating and enigmatic figures of early 18th-century European history. French writer Voltaire dubbed him 'the Lion of the North'. Acceding to the throne in 1697 at the tender age of 15, he had bitten off rather more than he could chew by taking on Russia and spent the following six years in exile in and around present-day Turkey. It was here that he acquired a taste for the local cuisine and, when he returned to Sweden in 1714, he brought back a recipe for *köfte*, or spiced lamb and beef meatballs, which have since evolved into the Swedish staple *köttbullar*.

This is my take on the classic, a wilder version inspired by Swedish chef Niklas Ekstedt, who also uses venison. I've also offered a plant-based option. The dandelion root coffee is completely optional. It adds depth of flavour, is a brilliant liver tonic (so a great nod to good health) and it's also there as a wink back to King Charles XII, whose other foodie import from Turkey to Sweden was coffee. Apparently, the young king used to eat his meatballs alongside a pot of coffee.

SERVES 4

For the hedgerow honey
2 tbsp dried elderberries and/or hawthorn berries, or fresh/frozen
    lingonberries or cranberries
2 tbsp honey

For the meatballs
200g cooked mushrooms, or 50g dried mushrooms, soaked in water
    to rehydrate, both finely chopped
4 garlic cloves, finely grated
6 finely crushed juniper berries, or allspice berries (optional)
1 tsp finely ground dandelion root coffee (optional, see page 296)
½ tsp freshly ground black pepper
½ tsp fennel seeds
generous grating of nutmeg
1 tsp thyme leaves, or rosemary leaves
400g minced wild venison, or 400g sprouted Puy lentils (see page 66),
    or cooked Puy lentils
sea salt
2 tbsp ghee (for homemade, see page 214), or coconut oil

For the parsnip mash
1kg parsnips
2 tbsp butter, or olive oil, plus more (optional) for the peels
1 garlic clove
finely grated zest and juice of 1 lemon
freshly ground black pepper

To serve (optional)
drizzle of olive oil, or herb oil
pine needles, or dill (fresh or dried)

Make the hedgerow honey. Place the fruit in a saucepan with enough water to just cover and cook over a medium heat until the fruit is plump and most of the water has been absorbed, 2–3 minutes. Take off the heat and fold the fruit and 1 tbsp of the cooking liquid through the honey in a heatproof bowl. You can leave the fruit loose in the honey and drizzle both over the meatballs, or blend them together and press them through a sieve for a smoother sauce. You can use any strained solids on porridge, toast or in a cake or flapjack recipe.

To give the meatballs a luxurious, melt-in-your mouth texture, it's best to blend the ingredients. Blend the mushrooms, garlic and all the flavourings in a food processor, or with a stick blender, then blend in the meat or lentils and season with salt. Once blended, shape the mixture into walnut-sized balls, you should get 12–16 meatballs. Place on a plate and chill them for 15 minutes before cooking.

Preheat the oven to 200°C/190°C fan. Set a large roasting tin on the top shelf to heat up.

Add the ghee or coconut oil to the warmed roasting tin. Add the chilled meatballs, gently rolling through the fat to lightly baste. Bake for 20 minutes on the top shelf, or until nicely coloured.

Meanwhile, scrub the parsnips, then peel, reserving the peelings. Roast the parsnip peels with 1 tbsp butter or oil, salt and pepper while the meatballs cook: they'll happily roast until crisp in a tray set on a shelf in the oven under the meatballs and they make a brilliant garnish for the final dish.

Chop the parsnips into about 3cm pieces. Pop them in a pan with a good pinch of salt and pepper. Cover with water and cook for 15–20 minutes or until tender. Drain the parsnips, saving a mug of the cooking water. Peel the garlic clove. Return the parsnips to the pan and add the butter or olive oil, peeled garlic, lemon zest, a squeeze of lemon juice, a pinch of salt and a good grinding of pepper. Mash until creamy and smooth, or whizz in a food processor or blender. Add some of the cooking water or more lemon juice, if needed. Adjust the seasoning to taste.

Serve the meatballs on the mash with a drizzle of the hedgerow honey, a little oil and a scattering of crisp parsnip peelings and pine needles and/or dill. Delicious with a side of seasonal greens. Steamed or blanched kale with garlic, lemon and olive oil, and a spoonful of Levantine garlic paste (see page 216), would be perfect.

SWEET POTATO DAUPHINOISE

This is a decadent twist on the indulgent garlicky, creamy potato-based dish, in which the exotic richness of coconut milk and warming curry spices replace cream. Sweet potatoes (or squash) are the perfect sponges to soak in all the indulgent flavours, making this a comfort dish in all respects, as it will leave you wildly satisfied – both taste buds and tummy – without feeling over-indulged. This dish also works beautifully with thick slices or wedges of cauliflower.

I once had leftovers of this and my son mixed it with noodles and lobster for the most decadent dish ever. I would purposefully have that combination of leftover dauphinoise, lobster and noodles again! Crab meat would also be a nice, sea-kissed addition for that extra layer.

SERVES 4

4 sweet potatoes, or 1 medium squash
500ml veg or chicken stock, cold or lightly warmed (not hot), plus more (optional) if needed
400ml can of coconut milk, plus more (optional) if needed
1 tbsp mild curry powder, or Winter five spice (see page 230)
4 garlic cloves, finely chopped or grated
thumb of root turmeric, finely grated, or 1 tsp ground turmeric
thumb of root ginger, finely grated
50g cashews, crushed
12 curry leaves (optional)
sea salt and freshly ground black pepper

Preheat the oven to 200°C/190°C fan.

Slice the sweet potatoes into 1cm-thick rounds, or squash in 1–2cm-thick slices. Arrange the slices in a dish measuring about 27 × 21cm, or 25cm in diameter, seasoning well as you go. If the dauphinoise lies 3–4cm deep, that will help it to cook evenly and pick up a well caramelised top.

In a bowl, whisk together the stock, coconut milk, curry powder, garlic, turmeric and ginger. Add a good pinch of pepper and a pinch of salt. Pour this over until the vegetables are covered; you want about 1cm of liquid over the top of the veg, so add more stock and/or coconut milk if needed (if you have too much liquid, save it for another dish, as the amount you need will vary depending on the size of the vegetables and the dimensions of the dish). Finish with another hit of pepper and slide into the oven to bake for 45 minutes.

Remove from the oven, sprinkle the cashews and curry leaves, if using, over the top and return to the oven for a further 5–10 minutes, or until the cashews are lightly toasted and the dish is golden, bubbly and tender right the way through. Lovely with a simple salad, greens and a side dish of rice or noodles (or see recipe introduction).

A LAMB STEW 'PRESCRIPTION'

Sun Simiao, a scientist who lived during the Tang Dynasty (618–907), believed food was medicine. This recipe is inspired by a soup in his book *Beiji Qianjin Yaofang* or 'Prescriptions for Emergencies Worth a Thousand Pieces of Gold'. Beyond its healing properties, it provides delicious winter warming comfort. Angelica root has a strong, sweet, earthy flavour with a bitter aftertaste and invigorating warmth that lingers on the tongue.

SERVES 4–6

750g–1kg chopped lamb, hogget, or mutton, or loin chops
20g dried angelica root, or *dāng guī* (optional, see page 127)
500g carrots and/or parsnips
2 leeks, or 8 spring onions
thumb of root ginger
4 garlic cloves
1 tbsp ghee (for homemade, see page 214), or coconut oil
1 tsp Sichuan peppercorns
2 cinnamon sticks
2 star anise
4 tbsp tamari, or soy sauce
1.5 litres Gut healing veg stock, Herb broth (see pages 104 and 108), or water
1–2 tbsp rice vinegar, or apple cider vinegar
1 tbsp honey
400g Swiss chard, or winter greens, sliced into 5cm-wide ribbons
sea salt and freshly ground black pepper

Preheat the oven to 200°C/190°C fan. Rinse the meat and pat dry, then dust a pinch of salt and a good grinding of pepper over. Soak the angelica in a small bowl of cold water for 5 minutes.

Scrub the carrots and/or parsnips clean; peel if the skin is thick and woody, otherwise leave it on. Cut them into 1cm-thick slices. Thinly slice the leeks (use their dark greens, too) or, if using spring onions, cut them into 3cm pieces. Give them a good clean. Cut the ginger and garlic into fine slices.

Set a large, lidded casserole dish over a medium-low heat. Add the ghee or coconut oil and the lamb. Let it brown for 5 minutes on each side. Stir in the leeks or spring onions, ginger, garlic and spices. Gently cook, stirring, for 2–3 minutes or until the spices are fragrant and the vegetables soften. Add the tamari or soy sauce, then add the carrots and/or parsnips, stock and angelica along with its soaking liquid. Pop a lid on, then slide into the oven and cook for 2 hours or until the meat is fall-apart tender.

Fold in the vinegar and honey. Taste and adjust the seasoning as needed, then fold the greens through. They should cook in the residual heat, but place over a medium heat, if needed, to help them soften. Serve warm.

Winter is the natural season for eating lamb

If you want to eat lamb that has been reared in a natural seasonal cycle, with high animal welfare and a green stamp of approval for sustainability – as well as richer flavour and nutritional benefits – you should look to eat it later in the year, when the animal is six to nine months old. This takes a lamb born in the British springtime into late autumn or early winter. Or you can opt for animals that had even richer lives (and lapped up more nutrients) by trying hogget (a sheep that is one or two years old) or mutton (typically two to three years old, sometimes more).

Health philosophies in traditional Chinese medicine gravitate towards eating lamb in the colder months. In China, when the temperatures drop, a popular phrase is, 'It's cold now, let's eat lamb,' because lamb falls under the category of warming foods which help the 'yang' energy. Supposedly, this can reduce cold symptoms such as a cold body, clammy skin, stomach ache, lack of energy and sore joints.

STORE CUPBOARD

REMEDIES

Archaeologists have discovered hundreds
of inscribed bamboo slips from the Han period
(202 BC–220 AD) giving information about
preserving foods, highlighting methods such
as salting, sun-drying and pickling.

The principles around preserving are simple. In most respects, you're driving off any moisture that can lead to spoilage, or adding elements such as salt, sugar or vinegar to create a pH so low (acidic) that no bacteria can grow. Traditions around preserving, however, give extraordinary insights into histories, cultures and their ingenuity in the fight to survive and progress. Often – or, at least, traditionally – the art can be a way to bring family and community together, such as kimchi-making traditions in Korea or miso-making in Japan (see pages 205 and 115), both winter rituals.

What I love about preserving is that each jar is a like a time capsule, a memory captured, that you cherish with all your senses at a later date.

PRESERVING MEMORIES

This chapter celebrates the art of preserving in a bid to ensure skills are not lost, but also to honour even the smallest winter gluts you might have in your own kitchen, such as ribs stripped from kale leaves that took months to grow and are full of nutrients. Why throw them away when you can turn them into a fabulous little relish that will take only minutes to make? When the garden's full of herbs, you'll never regret picking extra to dry for a day when you've got nothing fresh to add fragrance to a dish. Dried herbs can be more intense, and those you preserved yourself will always be fresher than anything you can buy.

My granny always preserved the gluts from my grandad's buoyant Texas garden, and, when we came for dinner, she had the table full of nibbles laid out in an instant, plucking from her supply of jars. Her beetroot pickles were my favourite.

You could even argue that preserving food had a bolstering effect on human civilisation itself: without bundling abundance away for the lean times, we might not have survived.

MEXICAN TACO PICKLES

In Mexico, wise *abuelitas* (grannies) ferment red onions in honey to make a mild, sweet cough syrup which is said to perform magic on sore throats, colds and coughs. We are only pickling them here, but nevertheless red onions have a particular advantage over brown or white, as they score higher levels of antioxidants, in particular quercetin. The benefits of quercetin are reduced inflammation, a boost to the immune system and an ability to kill bad bacteria.

Not only is this amazingly simple Mexican pickle easy to make, it has the boosted health benefits of being steeped in vitamin C-rich citrus, and I've married it with warming antiviral cloves, which lend a subtly sweet, aromatic note, while the coriander seeds complement the citrus and effortlessly add another layer of complexity.

I nearly always have a jar of these in my refrigerator, as the tickled-pink onions add an instant element of texture and flavour to salads, or indeed to any dish. Beyond tacos, they're brilliant added to simple dal, grilled fish and so much more.

Sterilising jars ensures a longer shelf life for all your condiments. Wash the jars in hot soapy water, then place in a preheated oven at 100°C/90°C fan for 10 minutes or until fully dried and warm to touch. Meanwhile, place the jar lids in a saucepan of water and bring to the boil, then remove from the heat, extract the lids with tongs and shake dry before placing on the filled jars. It's important that the jars are at the same temperature as the contents you're putting in them, so if you're bundling raw veg, or anything at room temperature, into sterilised jars, ensure they cool fully first. If you're filling with boiling hot ingredients, fill the hot jars right to the top and seal immediately.

SERVES 4–6

1 large red onion, halved and finely sliced
200ml freshly squeezed lime juice, and/or orange juice (a mix of lime and blood orange juice is my favourite here)
1½ tsp sea salt
½ tsp coriander seeds
4 whole cloves

Place the onion in a sieve. Pour boiling water over, then rinse with cold water.

Mix the citrus juice and salt in a bowl. Place the rinsed onions in a lidded jar and pour the salted citrus mix over. Add the spices.

Let the onions marinate for 30 minutes before serving, or store in the refrigerator for up to 1 month.

RHUBARB PICKLED GINGER

Traditional recipes for Japanese pickled ginger include the mingling of a red shiso leaf or two to tickle the rhizome pink. Shiso has a wonderful aniseed-rich flavour that sits somewhere between basil and star anise. Any of those flavourings would be delicious additions to this simple pickle, but for a hint of rouge, I've assimilated rhubarb into the mix.

Beyond vanity, rhubarb's inclusion stems from ancient Chinese medicine. Its healing powers can be traced back to a 270 BC tome on herbal medicine called *Shen Nong Ben Cao Jing*, in which rhubarb roots are noted for their antibacterial and anti-tumour qualities. The stems are also rich in the same qualities and their colour denotes the presence of anthocyanins, which are potent antioxidants for restoring cell health.

This delightful pickle celebrates a perfect flavour marriage. Retaining a Japanese twang, it's delicious served with rice, yet it has a far greater reach beyond the realm of sushi sidekick. I love it with grilled mackerel, even more so when the fish has been basted with Black garlic teriyaki (see page 210). It also adds warmth to salads and is exceptional married with beetroot in any guise, or with Maple miso roast cauliflower (see page 82).

**MAKES ABOUT 150G
(6–8 SERVINGS)**

small rhubarb stick
5cm piece of root ginger, or to taste
100ml apple cider vinegar
50ml water
1–2 tbsp honey, or maple syrup, or to taste
½–1 tsp tamari, or to taste
1 star anise, or 1 shiso leaf (optional)

Slice the rhubarb into 3cm chunks, then into little matchsticks. Peel and cut the ginger into similar-sized matchsticks. You want 2 parts rhubarb to 1 part ginger, more or less. Pile into a saucepan.

Add the remaining ingredients. Warm over a medium heat for 3 minutes, or just until the rhubarb and ginger have softened slightly and all the flavours have mingled.

Taste and tweak to your liking: sweeten if you like, or add more ginger or tamari for piquancy or salt. This will keep for 2 weeks in the refrigerator.

CARROT MISOZUKE

Misozuke are Japanese-style pickles fermented in miso. Not only do you get the perks of a pickle that's rich in protein and probiotics, but you also receive all the benefits of raw veg, as this is a completely raw pickle softened only by time... in this case, just the passing of a few days.

Once the veg is pickled, you can use the miso as the base for soups, just as you would straight miso from a jar, but with the added flavours from the spices and carrots.

MAKES 250G

100g unpasteurised miso
2 tbsp rice wine vinegar, sake, or lime juice
1 garlic clove, peeled and finely chopped
1 tbsp finely grated root ginger
pinch of chilli flakes
200g carrots

Put all the ingredients apart from the carrots into a shallow dish with a lid. Mix well.

Thinly slice the carrots, or cut into batons. Fold the carrots through the miso mix.

Cover with a lid and ferment in the refrigerator for at least 3 days before eating; they will happily keep fermenting there for up to 1 month.

Use the leftover marinade as you would normal miso paste, to make soup, or add flavour and depth to other dishes.

RAYU

This traditional Japanese chilli oil has always been the main lure for me to order ramen, as it's the classic accompaniment. It's also lovely doused over any sort of eggs, drizzled over fish or roasted lamb, or used to pep up most grain-based dishes, from a simple steamy bowl of rice to a hearty barley pilaf. Rayu also makes a great spicy contrast to Kefir labneh (see page 256) when swirled through it and served as a dip.

MAKES 200G

1 garlic clove, finely chopped
150ml toasted sesame oil
1 tbsp almonds, cashews, or peanuts (optional)
1–2 tbsp sesame seeds
1 tbsp chilli flakes
1 tbsp tamari, or soy sauce
strip of dried orange zest (whole or crushed to a powder), optional
pinch of sea salt

Set a small frying pan over a medium heat. Add the garlic with a pinch of salt and 1 tbsp of the sesame oil.

Gently cook the garlic to help crisp it up, without burning it or allowing the oil to get to smoking point. Spoon the toasted garlic into the sterilised jar or bottle (see page 186) you are going to use to house your rayu.

Set the pan back over a medium heat. Finely chop or crush the almonds, cashews or peanuts, if using, and add to the pan. Gently toast until just golden. Fold in the sesame seeds – you can use 2 tbsp if not using nuts – and give them a toasty kiss of heat.

Spoon the toasted nuts, if using, and sesame seeds into the rayu jar or bottle. Add the chilli flakes, tamari or soy sauce, the remaining sesame oil and strip of dried orange zest, if using. Give it a good stir or shake to mingle all the flavours. The chilli flavour and colour will start to shine through after 2–3 days, but you can use it straight away if you're keen.

It will happily keep for 3 months at room temperature.

KALE RIB RELISH

This has been a winter staple in my kitchen for decades. It was created to harness the raw goodness of cruciferous offcuts such as the woody ribs from kale or the leggy stems from purple-sprouting or Tenderstem broccoli. You can easily scale the recipe up or down. Embracing these green, leggy morsels helps capture a rich source of a powerful antioxidant called sulforaphane, which many studies show helps tame the growth of cancer cells. Here, their benefits are enhanced with the raw garlic and curry spices. This little relish transforms usually-composted kale ribs into something rather gorgeous dolloped alongside Ligurian leek pancakes (see page 62), or with a simple dal.

MAKES ABOUT 150G
(ABOUT 6 × 1 TSP SERVINGS)

10 kale ribs (the bit that's left after you've stripped off the leaves), or broccoli stem offcuts
1 garlic clove
1 tsp mild curry powder
½ tsp coriander seeds and/or fennel seeds
½ tsp finely grated root ginger
pinch of chilli flakes (optional)
1 tsp sea salt
200ml water
3–4 bay leaves

Finely chop the kale ribs, or thinly slice or chop the broccoli stem offcuts. Peel and slice the garlic. Bundle the greens and garlic into a sterilised jar (see page 188) with the curry powder, seeds, ginger, chilli, if using, and salt.

Pour in half the measured water. Nestle the bay leaves on top, providing a 'cap' to keep the veg under the brine. Add the remaining water, filling the jar until it comes right to the top.

Secure with a lid and let it ferment at room temperature for 2 weeks. In this time, the nutritional value of the stalks or stems will increase and the veg will have also softened and married with all the spices. If you notice the jar hissing, it will need 'burping': just unseal the lid briefly to release the build-up of gas.

Eat straight away, or store in the refrigerator for up to 1 year.

PRESERVED CITRUS

One of the easiest and most delicious ways to preserve citrus. The traditional variety used in Morocco is citron beldi, which is small and highly aromatic. Bergamot lemons, which are larger but with a similar fragrance, are also favoured, but regular lemons work beautifully, too, as do Seville, blood or navel oranges, limes, kumquats, limequats... and the list goes on. You can jumble them all up in one jar, too: they look pretty and offer a pick-and-mix of subtly different flavours.

MAKES ABOUT A 200G JAR

200g citrus (see recipe introduction)
30g sea salt
good pinch of fennel seeds
1 cinnamon stick, snapped into a few pieces
a few cardamom pods, bruised
several bay leaves

Wash the citrus and cut it into bite-sized pieces. Put the salt and spices in a bowl with the citrus and scrunch everything together to release some of the citrus juices, which will help dissolve the salt and create a brine.

Pack the citrus into a sterilised jar (see page 188). Press down, leaving about 1cm of head room. Nestle an overlapping tapestry of bay leaves on top, providing a 'cap' to keep the fruit under the brine. Top up with water, filling right to the top.

Seal the jar with a lid. Leave in a dark, cool place to mature, shaking often and checking to ensure the fruit is always covered in brine. If it's not, make up a brine solution using 100ml filtered or mineral water mixed with 4g sea salt and use it to top up the jars.

They'll be ready in about 3 months, but will keep for years; I find the longer you leave them, the better. Store in the refrigerator once opened and use within a few months, remembering that they'll store for longer if you keep them covered with brine.

PRESERVED CITRUS PASTE

I've been seeing these jars of golden, umami-rich citrus paste around a lot; I first spied it in an upmarket deli in New York. Think of it like a lemon miso: it has all the complexity and salty moreishness of the fermented soy bean paste, but with a zesty, lemony tang. It's a bit like Japanese yuzu sauce married with umeboshi paste. Arguably, it's easier to use than whole or chopped preserved lemons: you can just dollop a flavour-packed pop into dressings, soups and dips, or stir it through rice-, grain- and pulse-based dishes for instant delicious-factor amplification. Citrus are immunity-boosting, vitamin C powerhouses, helping your body fight infection, and they also promote collagen, which is both soothing for the gut and supports skin health from the effects of ageing.

MAKES 200G

200g preserved citrus (for homemade, see page 197)
juice from 1–2 lemons, or other citrus (optional)

Remove the preserved citrus from the jar. Roughly chop and try to extract any pips you come across. Blend the preserved citrus (zest, pith and flesh for maximum flavour, body and benefits), adding enough preserved citrus brine or juice to create a smooth lemon curd-like paste. Fresh citrus juice will make the paste a little fresher and less salty, without affecting its shelf life.

Spoon the paste into a clean lidded jar (no need to sterilise, but ensure that the jar is clean). Secure the lid and store in the refrigerator for up to 6 weeks.

TURMERIC AND BLACK PEPPER VINEGAR

Turmeric in any form is a gem for the human body, due to its numerous health benefits. Ayurveda, traditional Chinese and Siddha traditions revere its anti-inflammatory properties, which can aid in reducing the inflammation of tonsils, throat and knees and can offer relief from many other aches and pains. Gargling 1 tbsp of this vinegar mixed with 1 tbsp warm water can help relieve sore throats and aid good digestion, but this delicious brew can also be used to boost the flavour of dishes.

I love it dashed over dal before serving, or used with linseed oil (1 tbsp vinegar with 2 tbsp oil and 1 tsp raw honey) to make a dressing for winter leaves, or to finish roasted veg such as parsnips or potatoes, scattered with thyme leaves. You can also use it in place of the orange juice in Celeriac Seville ceviche (see page 74).

The best approach to this is to alternate using it as a vinegar and a turmeric pickle until you reach the end of the bottle, or you can strain the infused vinegar into a bottle and use the turmeric just as you would use root turmeric in any recipe.

**MAKES 200–250ML
(ABOUT 12 SERVINGS)**

100g root turmeric
250ml apple cider vinegar, plus more if needed
2 tsp honey, or maple syrup
½ tsp black peppercorns

Peel the turmeric and cut it into julienne strips for ease of getting it into the bottle (and ease of eating it as a pickle). Smaller pieces also result in a faster infusion.

Tuck the turmeric into a glass bottle. Mix the apple cider vinegar with the honey or maple syrup and pour into the bottle, ensuring the turmeric is fully covered (top up with vinegar, if needed).

Tip the black peppercorns into the mix. Seal and shake to help get the infusing process started. To maximise its benefits, allow the turmeric to infuse for at least 24 hours before using. You can leave the turmeric in the bottle, so long as it's covered.

The vinegar will keep indefinitely, but is best used within 1 year. The turmeric will keep for 6 months (or longer) if it's covered with vinegar: top up with vinegar if needed, to ensure it is always covered.

FOUR THIEVES VINEGAR

The benefits of steeping herbs in vinegar are vast. A variation of this mixture was used as a remedy in the Middle Ages, during the bubonic plague. Legend has it the name is attributable to four thieves in the south of France, who offered their curative recipe in exchange for redemption from robbing the dead. Their brew, to be fair, was an attempt to prevent further fatalities. Extracting the medicinal properties of herbs by steeping them in vinegar is a practice that reaches back to Hippocrates, who was aware of its potent effects.

Beyond the history and the name, what I love most about this infused vinegar is the flavour it produces. The lavender offers herbaceous notes which are surprisingly savoury. I love splashing it over L'escargot mushrooms (see page 86) or using it to marinate ribbons of carrots for a simple salad, which is lovely finished with Digestive dukkah (see page 226). As well as steeping the herbs in vinegar, I also like to dry a fresh bundle of lavender, rosemary, thyme and sage as a *herbes d'hiver* medley: my winter take on *herbes de Provence*.

MAKES 400ML

4 lavender sprigs
4 rosemary sprigs
4 thyme sprigs
4 sage sprigs
1 garlic clove
1 cinnamon stick and/or 4 cloves (optional)
400ml cider vinegar

Place the herbs, garlic and spices in a clean bottle. Cover with the vinegar. Let it infuse for at least 24 hours before using.

This will keep indefinitely, but it's best to remove the herbs, or strain the infused vinegar into a fresh bottle and discard the herbs, after 1 month.

PROBIOTIC RANCH DRESSING

Winter offers one of the most abundant arrays of salad leaves, mostly on the wildly flavourful and punchy side, with warming mustards and beautifully blushing bitter chicory (to grow your own, see page 67).

This is a brilliant dressing for such leaves, or indeed for any winter veg. It is inspired by an American classic recipe, but features probiotic-rich kefir in place of the traditional buttermilk, as well as digestive-friendly spices and thyme, which is a brilliant herb for keeping bad bugs at bay. Beyond using it as a dressing, you can also strain it through muslin, labneh-style (see page 256) and use it as a spread or a dip.

MAKES 200ML (4 SERVINGS)

200g kefir
1 tbsp olive oil (omit this if you plan to strain it to make labneh, see recipe introduction)
finely grated zest of 1 lemon
1 tsp cumin seeds, or caraway seeds
1 tsp fresh thyme leaves, or ½ tsp dried thyme leaves, or to taste
sea salt and freshly ground black pepper

Pop the kefir, olive oil, if using, lemon zest, cumin or caraway seeds, thyme leaves and a pinch of salt and pepper into a bowl or jam jar and shake or whisk to combine.

Taste and tweak the seasoning, or add more herbs, as you like. This will keep for 1 week in the refrigerator.

Kimjang, the seasonal ritual of kimchi

Some time during November, or maybe early December, depending on the temperatures, Korean families will set aside a weekend for *kimjang*. This is an annual kimchi-making tradition shaped around the first frost, the cold of which teases out the sweet notes in the blowsy, water-rich and light-hued Chinese leaf that forms the base of most kimchi.

In search of stories around this tradition, I met the wonderful Rebecca Ghim, founder and director of a small kimchi operation in London called The Ferm. Rebecca is from Gwangju, South Korea and came to London to do an MA in Design for Social Innovation and Sustainable Futures. Her studies inspired research around food waste and food insecurity, as well as anthropology. It led Rebecca's thinking back to her granny, who orchestrated her family each year through the tradition of making kimchi, an art that not only preserved seasonal bounty, but also culture.

The kimchi made by Rebecca's granny is a true form of edible art. The process begins in the late summer, when the persimmons on her beloved tree mature. These are frozen in anticipation of *kimjang*, to provide a fruity note to the kimchi as well as add sugars to aid the fermentation process, and pectin, which will help to bring the chilli paste together.

Every region and each individual family bring something bespoke to their approach to kimchi. Rebecca's family seem to have layers upon layers of storytelling and ingredients enriching their recipe, including a special liqueur called *cheong*, made by fermenting a local plum with sugar when it ripens in late summer and put aside until the kimchi is made at the end of the year. They also add several different types of dried fish and fish sauces to their kimchi, to make it unique.

Rebecca's London version of kimchi is made with restaurant industry waste, with a focus on harnessing an excess of cauliflower leaves that normally end up in compost bins, which she uses in place of Chinese leaf. To create a vegan offering, she swaps the fish for shiitake mushrooms and seaweed. These are infused in the brine, which is poured over the chilli-pasted coated veg to marinate before it's all packed into jars to ferment.

The ritual is such a potent part of Rebecca's cultural and family history and it's the thing she missed most when she first left Korea. I love her story about her time in Los Angeles, where she first lived abroad. She brought two suitcases with her: one for clothes and the other packed with enough kimchi to see her through the whole year, until her next visit home.

CHORIZO KIMKRAUT

The following recipe has become the signature kimchi made at River Cottage's Park Farm in Devon, where we use autumn produce plucked from the garden to make enough kimchi to see us through winter. It's called kimkraut, as it has a nod to kimchi spicing, but it's finely shredded like a sauerkraut.

There are so many things I love about this recipe. I think the first is the inclusion of squash grown in the market garden and the addition of Jerusalem artichokes from the kitchen garden, which give it a prebiotic boost. But what makes it unique is the carefully chosen spices themed around a River Cottage favourite: chorizo. Because this kraut is fermented, just like the cured meat version, it is the perfect plant-based alternative.

It's a truly flexible ferment, too, which you can adapt, swapping in veg that are in abundance near you. Often, when I'm on a fridge-clearing mission (especially pre-holiday), I literally bundle just about everything from my veg drawer into a batch of kimchi, which then awaits my return, giving me nourishing veg in the absence of fresh produce. This is exactly why kimchi has such important cultural connotations: not only are you preserving veg while it's in abundance, but you're enhancing its health benefits, as the fermentation process increases nutrients – vitamin C alone can increase by up to 50 per cent – while amplifying flavour.

Any cabbage is fine – apart from red, which just looks wrong! – and Chinese leaf or cauliflower leaves are both ideal.

MAKES ABOUT 1 LITRE

500g cabbage (see recipe introduction)
350g squash, pumpkin, or carrots
150g Jerusalem artichokes, or beetroot
1 small onion, red or white
5 garlic cloves
1 tbsp smoked paprika
2 tsp ground cumin
1 tsp caraway seeds
1 tsp thyme leaves
good crack of freshly ground black pepper
about 20g sea salt
4 per cent brine (made by mixing 4g sea salt with 100ml water)

Strip a few large outer leaves from the cabbage and set aside. Trim the base from the cabbage, then quarter it and thinly shred the leaves. Scrub the squash, pumpkin or carrots and Jerusalem artichokes or beetroot clean and coarsely grate them all. Halve, peel and finely slice the red onion. Peel and finely grate or chop the garlic.

Mix all the veg, garlic and spices, thyme and pepper together.

Weigh the mix and add 2g sea salt for every 100g of prepared ingredients. Mix the salt through and pack into clean, dry 500g jars, adding it little by little and and packing down each layer as you go. It's important to exclude as much air as possible during this process. Fill the jar to the line just below where the lid will sit.

Cover the mixture with the reserved large cabbage leaves and press this leaf cap down. Top up with the brine, filling the jars right to the very top.

Screw an airtight lid on the jars and set them on a plate to catch any juices that bubble over during fermentation (caused by the build-up of carbon dioxide, as the good bacteria consume the natural sugars in the veg).

Ferment at room temperature, out of direct sunlight, for 2 weeks. If you notice the jar hissing, it will need 'burping': just unseal the lid briefly to release the build-up of gas.

Eat, or store in the refrigerator for up to 6 months, ensuring it is always covered with brine and the lid is airtight (in theory, it'll keep longer, but 6 months is a good marker). Should it start to look or smell off, discard it.

Benefits of black garlic

If you were to eat a black garlic clove while blindfolded, you might think you were eating a balsamic-flavoured jelly sweet. The dark, sticky cloves are soft and tangy, with only the faintest hint of garlic. Koreans have been creating this highly prized ingredient for as long as four thousand years. In Thailand, black garlic is believed to increase longevity, and there it features in everything from chocolates to sauces. As well as hints of balsamic, black garlic also has the strong sweet-and-tangy notes of tamarind, for which it makes a good swap.

Black garlic is not a special variety of the allium, rather it's created by slowly ageing regular garlic bulbs, effectively fermenting them by cooking them at a very low heat over the course of sixty to ninety days. The bulbs are kept in a humidity-controlled environment at a temperature of 60–77°C. There are no additives, preservatives or burning of any kind. The enzymes that give fresh garlic its sharpness break down throughout this process and the cloves are transformed from their sharp flavour, white colour and crunchy texture to sticky, date-like black nuggets.

The health benefits are also transformed. The process gives black garlic a higher content of antioxidants, particularly a compound called S-allyl cysteine, which has been shown to have anti-inflammatory and anti-cancer properties. It also has more amino acids and minerals than raw garlic.

BLACK GARLIC TERIYAKI

One of the oldest known references to teriyaki sauce is from the Edo period in Japan (1603–1867). Recipes vary quite significantly, with original versions composed simply of soy sauce, mirin and sake. The latter two caramelise on cooking, creating a sticky, slightly sweet glaze balanced with deeply savoury, salty notes.

Many modern versions migrated west via Hawaii, where sugar was used in place of, or in addition to, mirin and sake. My black garlic take on teriyaki veers far from both traditional and modern renditions, yet triggers familiar flavour, texture and appearance cues. It's also a deliciously straightforward medley of ingredients, the hero being black garlic, which gives the sauce a health boost as well as teriyaki's iconic caramelised sugar notes.

This is delicious used just like regular teriyaki as a glaze for meat or fish before and/or after grilling. I love it brushed over grilled mackerel, roasted purple-sprouting broccoli or grilled aubergine, just after grilling, which ensures the nutrients in the sauce aren't decreased by heat. It's also wonderful tossed with noodles, stirred into rice or added to Miso mushroom porridge (see page 34).

The dark, aromatic, papery skins of black garlic not only have flavour, they also house many of the benefits found in the garlic cloves themselves. If you have a coffee grinder, you can pulse the dry skins into a powder: they are brilliant added to Mushroom furikake (see page 224) or used as a spice just as you'd use garlic powder or any other ground spice. The flavour is like a toasted garlic balsamic: it's lovely dusted over flatbreads or rice.

**MAKES 150G
(4–6 SERVINGS)**

50g black garlic cloves
50ml toasted sesame oil
2 tbsp tamari, or soy sauce, or to taste
1 tbsp apple cider vinegar, or to taste

Blend all the ingredients until smooth. Taste and adjust the salt or sour levels by adding more tamari or soy sauce or apple cider vinegar.

Spoon into a sterilised lidded container (see page 188) and store in the refrigerator for up to 2 months.

GOLDEN BUTTER

This is my mother's cure-all remedy for colds and flu, a simple trinity of ingredients that seem to be made for each other both taste- and health-wise. Turmeric features widely throughout this book, because of its potent anti-inflammatory properties. When our bodies are fighting illness – no matter what illness it is – inflammation occurs. Turmeric is brilliant for soothing the sudden swellings which lead to aches and pains, but to get the full benefits it needs to be paired with a healthy fat such as coconut oil (or olive oil, linseed oil or nuts). Without fat, the turmeric struggles to make it through the liver and stomach and into the small intestines, where it can be transferred to the blood. This pairing is what gave rise to the popularity of 'golden milk' or turmeric lattes, as the fats in the milk help the gilded root get into the bloodstream and work its magic.

The addition of black pepper further boosts absorption. Pairing black pepper with turmeric increases your body's ability to assimilate it by up to two thousand per cent.

Flavourwise, the trio – whipped into a golden butter – creates the most delicious boost for so many dishes, be it a simple bowl of steamed rice, an instant base for a turmeric latte, a plant-based spread for freshly baked bread (try it with Overnight five seed bread, see page 40), or as a rich swirl through freshly cooked oats; try it in place of tahini in Tahini pear porridge (see page 24).

**MAKES 120G
(8–10 SERVINGS)**

100g coconut oil
1 tbsp ground turmeric
1 tsp freshly ground black pepper

Mix all the ingredients in a sterilised jar (see page 188). The coconut oil will soften as you stir.

Store in the refrigerator for up to 3 months. You can keep it at room temperature, but I always note a subtle change in flavour (and not for the better) so I feel it is wiser to store it in the refrigerator.

GOLDEN CHAI LATTE

To use this butter for a golden chai latte, warm 250ml milk of your choice in a saucepan and whisk in 1 tbsp Golden butter, and – for additional flavour and nourishment – add 1 tsp Masala chai (see page 231), or more Golden butter, spice or a little honey, to taste.

GHEE

Ghee is similar to clarified butter: all the milk solids are removed, but it's cooked just a little longer, allowing the solids on the base of the pan to caramelise, giving a nutty flavour.

Ghee has been enjoyed in the Middle East and Asia for thousands of years and is used in Ayurveda and other healing practices.

It has a high smoke point. That means it's a great cooking fat and you can fry with it. It's also nutrient-dense, containing vitamins A, K2 and gut-healing butyric acid.

MAKES ABOUT 200G

250g butter, preferably unsalted

Place the butter in a saucepan and gently cook over a low heat until it has melted and started to simmer.

As it reaches a simmer, the butter will separate. First, a layer of foam forms on the top and it'll sputter a little, which is the water evaporating. Skim the foamy layer off with a spoon, getting as much of the white frothy or creamy bits off as you can while trying not to mix it into the golden liquid (which is the ghee) below. The idea is to try to remove the creamy milk solids from the golden translucent fat, as milk solids burn, whereas fat can tolerate higher temperatures (and has a longer shelf life). The skimmed-off milk solids are worth keeping to use in baking, or to stir through cooked veg.

The whole process of gently simmering the butter, allowing the milk solids to rise to the top and skimming them off, takes 10–15 minutes. Once you have removed most of the white solids, turn off the heat and let it cool for a couple of minutes, then strain through muslin or a clean tea towel and transfer to a lidded jar. You will have about 200g of ghee.

The ghee will become opaque and light yellow as it cools. Seal with a lid once fully cold and store in the refrigerator for up to 6 weeks.

LEVANTINE GARLIC PASTE

The term *levant* is a French word which means 'rising' and refers to the rising of the Sun in the east. Geographically speaking, the reference is a nod to the Mediterranean countries east of Italy, such as Syria, Lebanon and Israel. This region shares and celebrates a culinary staple called *toum*, which is like French aïoli but – happily for those who don't eat eggs – is a simplified plant-based version featuring three exceptionally healthy ingredients: raw garlic, lemon juice and olive oil. Some recipes call for milder seed oils, so do feel free to swap some of the olive oil for any other oils you favour, but I love using a good new season's olive oil.

In the Middle East, the paste is paired with artichokes, just as aïoli is in France, as well as with chicken and fries. I actually love keeping a pot of this in the refrigerator to use as an instant flavour boost for a simple side of steamed seasonal greens such as kale or broccoli. It's also a great base for salad dressings.

Soak the garlic cloves in iced water for a few minutes for a less potent taste. Make sure to dry them thoroughly afterwards, though, if you do this.

MAKES ABOUT 150G

5 large garlic cloves
pinch of sea salt
2 tsp lemon juice
100ml olive oil
2 tsp cold water

Finely grate the garlic cloves. Add a pinch of salt and whisk it into the garlic.

Whisk in 1 tsp of the lemon juice, then gradually start blending in the oil, little by little, vigorously whisking with each addition, adding the remaining lemon juice after you have whisked in one-quarter of the oil, 1 tsp of water after about half the oil has been added, and again adding 1 tsp of water after three-quarters of the oil has been incorporated. You should end up with a light, creamy-white garlicky paste akin to mayonnaise.

Once made, spoon into a sterilised lidded jar (see page 188) and store in the refrigerator for up to 1 month.

MAYAN PEPITA PESTO

This is a simplified version of a Yucatan pumpkin seed condiment called *sikil pak*. It's a little bit like a guacamole and can be served in the same way. I love using it on Celeriac tacos (see page 164).

What's brilliant about this dip is the powerhouse partnering of winter healing ingredients. Pumpkin seeds are rich with zinc and evidence suggests that a boost of this mineral at the onset of a cold can shorten the duration of illness. Zinc also plays an important role in mental health, as does magnesium, of which pumpkin seeds are also a rich source. Paired with the infection-fighting magic of coriander leaves and garlic, as well as vitamin C-rich lime, you're on to a winner in every sense.

Beyond tacos and Mexican food, this pesto can be tossed with pasta or paired with potatoes. It's also lovely loosened with extra citrus as a sauce for fish, or swirled through pumpkin soup.

**MAKES ABOUT 100G
(4–6 SERVINGS)**

4 tbsp pumpkin seed butter
30g bunch of coriander
1 large garlic clove
2 limes, plus more lime juice if needed
pinch of sea salt
pinch of chilli flakes, or cayenne pepper (optional)
a little olive oil, or pumpkin seed oil

Measure the pumpkin seed butter. Finely chop the coriander (you can chop in the stems, too, so long as they're not too woody). Peel and finely chop or grate the garlic clove. Zest and juice the limes.

Blend everything together, adding the salt and chilli, if using, for a smooth pesto. Or, you can combine everything in a mortar and pestle, or on a chopping board and muddle together, for a more rustic texture.

Loosen with more lime juice, a little water, or some oil, if needed. Spoon into a lidded jar, cover with a thin gloss of oil, seal the jar and store in the refrigerator for up to 1 week.

PEASO

To truly connect with the seasons and our landscape, sourcing ingredients grown near us delivers the richest reciprocity. At River Cottage, the smallholding in Devon where I teach fermentation, we make miso collectively as a group using one of Britain's old-grown varieties of peas: 'Black Badger'. Not only do I love the narrative and locality, but the variety also smells like roasted hazelnuts and freshly baked chocolate cake when you cook it. The first time I cooked a batch for miso, I could have sworn there was a cake in the oven.

I urge you to do the same and find a variety of bean or pea which grows near you, to a make a miso that's truly a reflection of your time and space.

MAKES 1KG

300g dried Black Badger or carlin peas (see recipe introduction), chickpeas, fava beans, or yellow peas, or other local peas or beans
300g rice *koji* (see page 115)
75g sea salt, plus more to finish

Rinse the dried beans or peas and put them into a lidded pan. Cover with plenty of water and leave them to soak overnight.

Drain and rinse the peas or beans. Return them to the pan, cover with plenty of water and bring to the boil. Reduce the heat and cook for 45–60 minutes, stirring every 10 minutes, until the peas are soft enough to break between your thumb and forefinger without applying much pressure. (Or cook in a pressure cooker for 20 minutes.) Some varieties of pea might take longer to cook. If they are stubbornly failing to become soft, stir 1 tsp bicarbonate of soda into the simmering pan, which should help the peas to soften.

Meanwhile, put the *koji* and salt into a large bowl. With your hands, rub the *koji* with the salt until the grains are separated.

Drain the cooked peas or beans, saving a large cup of cooking water. Mash them in a food processor or with a potato masher, then add the *koji* and enough of the saved water to make a paste, mixing well.

Pack the mixture tightly into sterilised jars (see page 188) until you reach the top, ensuring there are no air pockets. Wipe away any excess paste and flatten the top of the paste. Sprinkle a little salt over the top. Cover with a couple of layers of baking parchment to keep the miso paste airtight and seal tightly with the lids.

Keep the miso in a cool, dark place for a minimum of 6 months or up to 2 years. The longer you leave it, the darker and richer it will become. Once opened, store in the refrigerator, where it will keep for years.

DASHI STOCK POWDER

Japanese soup often has an umami-rich foundation stock made with kombu seaweed and bonito fish flakes. This is known as *awase dashi*.

Buddhist monks seeking fish-free alternatives use dried shiitake mushrooms in a version known as Shojin or Zen stock (see page 106). Shiitake have flavour molecules called lenthionine, giving distinctive earthy, meaty, umami-rich flavours. The process of drying and rehydrating shiitakes increases the production of lenthionine, adding to the mushroom's popularity (it's the second most-cultivated mushroom in the world).

Use this as a base for other soups. You can use dashi stock powder in place of the seaweed and mushroom powder in Mushroom furikake (see page 224), as a seasoning for rice, noodles or grilled fish, or a rub for roast lamb. Or mix 1 tsp into 1 tbsp miso for instant miso soup stock cubes (a cube makes a bowl of soup): I freeze a tray of these for instant soup on hand.

MAKES 100G, (ENOUGH FOR 3 LITRES OF DASHI STOCK)

50g dried shiitake mushrooms, or the same weight of shiitake powder
30g kombu
15g nori or dulse seaweed (flakes are fine here)

Add the whole shiitake, if using, to a coffee grinder and grind to a powder. Transfer to a jar. Snip the kombu and nori or dulse (if it's in sheets) into pieces small enough to fit into a coffee grinder and pulse to a powder. Add to the ground shiitake mushrooms and store in a lidded jar for up to 1 year.

Use 1½ tsp stock powder for every 250ml of freshly boiled, slightly cooled water, or 1 tbsp for 500ml.

How to cook perfect rice

Rinse the rice to remove excess starches on the outside of the grains. If they're not washed away, they cause the rice to clump and become gummy as it cooks. A tip is to place the rice in a fine-meshed sieve over a large bowl and rinse until the water in the bowl runs clear.

Measure the appropriate water to rice ratio. For white rice, use double the weight of water to rice (so for 200g white rice, use 400ml water or stock). For brown rice, use three times the amount of liquid to rice (so for 200g brown rice, use 600ml water or stock).

Put the water and rice in a medium saucepan and stir in 1 tsp sesame oil, or whatever oil you have to hand (olive, coconut, or ghee).

Bring the water to the boil, then reduce the heat, cover the saucepan and simmer for 40 minutes for brown rice or 20 minutes for white rice, until the rice is tender. The grains should have absorbed the water and you usually see little indentations across the surface of the rice.

Turn off the heat. Let the pot sit, covered, for 10 minutes, before removing the lid and fluffing with a fork.

If not eating straight away, spoon the warm rice into a shallow dish and stir a few times to help it cool quickly. Cover and place in the refrigerator as soon as it has cooled. It will keep happily for 24 hours (cooked, cooled and reheated rice is healthier for your gut than freshly cooked, see page 154).

Ensure the rice is fully heated through before eating.

MUSHROOM FURIKAKE

A traditional Japanese condiment which is typically known as 'rice seasoning', furikake is usually composed of seaweed flakes, sesame seeds and something with an umami-rich depth such as powdered miso or tamari. I've gone for mushrooms, some of which have brilliant medicinal qualities (especially reishi, see page 278, shiitake and maitake). The seaweed offers an additional depth of flavour, as well as boosting the nutrient content of the condiment.

Beyond rice, this is delicious with eggs, dusted over roasted carrots or stir-fried purple-sprouting broccoli. I like to use it to finish the Maple miso roast cauliflower (see page 82).

MAKES ABOUT 100G

4 tbsp sesame seeds (I like a mix of white and black, but either is fine)
2 tbsp dried mushrooms, ground in a mortar and pestle or coffee grinder, or 1 tbsp mushroom powder
2 tbsp seaweed flakes (nori or dulse)
pinch of chilli flakes (optional)

Lightly toast the sesame seeds. Cool, then simply mix them with all the other ingredients.

Bundle into a jar, secure with a lid and store for up to 6 months. A good serving size is 1–2 tsp.

DIGESTIVE DUKKAH

Ancient Egyptians imbued their beloved spices with symbolism: cumin was representative of faithfulness, for example, while coriander was considered a token for love and passion. Marrying these spices led to the birth of dukkah. Fennel isn't classically incorporated, but I've added it to the mix because of a traditional Egyptian reverence for its medicinal qualities. In sesame's usual place, I've suggested sunflower seeds, which feed the good bacteria in our guts. This makes a brilliant finishing touch for just about every dish, from soups and salads to dips, it adds pizazz to roasted or steamed veg, or can be dusted over a humble bowl of rice, breakfast eggs or porridge.

MAKES 120G (6–8 SERVINGS)

4 tbsp sunflower seeds
1 tbsp cumin seeds
1 tbsp coriander seeds
1 tbsp fennel seeds
pinch of sea salt

Preheat the oven to 180°C/170°C fan. Set a baking tray in the oven to heat up.

Scatter the sunflower seeds on the hot tray and toast them for 10 minutes while you measure out the spices.

Add the spices to the tray, return it to the oven and straight away turn the oven off. Allowing the spices to lap up the residual warmth will help them to release all their oils and flavours without damaging their benefits with excessive heat.

Remove from the oven after 5–10 minutes and allow to cool fully, before mixing in the salt and spooning into a lidded jar.

The dukkah will store at room temperature for up to 6 months.

Winter warming herbs and spices

Funnily, I'd never really thought about the phrase 'spice up your life' until I started composing the list here. I realised that not only are the following herbs and spices brilliant for stimulating your digestive system – which helps you absorb more nutrients from food, thus supporting general health – but that they are also great for helping to keep bad bugs and infection at bay, as well as assisting with circulation to help keep you warm in cold weather.

CARAWAY   Caraway's winter bonus is its ability to help ease congestion. As an expectorant, it can aid in the elimination of phlegm.

CARDAMOM   This spice is known for high levels of concentrated cineole, another natural expectorant which helps stimulate the lungs to loosen congestion.

CAYENNE   A compound in cayenne called capsaicin can help increase body heat, with research nodding to its potential for treating hypothermia.

CINNAMON   The warming effect of cinnamon stimulates circulation and clears congestion. In Chinese medicine, it is used to treat an array of problems caused by coldness, such as cold limbs and poor digestion.

CLOVES   Cloves are rich in potent antioxidants such as eugenol, which supports cells and helps fight disease. The spice is particularly good at supporting the liver in eliminating toxins and at breaking down food to convert it into energy.

CORIANDER   Both coriander leaves and seeds are rich sources of vitamin C and iron, which both help to boost immunity. The herb and spice both also contain a natural chemical compound called dodecanal, which acts as a potent antibiotic.

CUMIN   Due to their antibacterial, anti-inflammatory properties, cumin seeds are an awesome home remedy for colds and coughs. The compounds in the seeds help to soothe inflamed muscles and boost immunity to fight infections.

DILL   Grown under cover, dill can be prolific in the winter and consuming it helps the body to eliminate toxins. It's also a rich source of B-complex vitamins that promote restful sleep.

ELDERBERRIES   The berries and flowers of elder are packed with antioxidants and vitamins that may boost the immune system. They could help tame inflammation, lessen stress and ease the symptoms of colds and flu.

FENNEL   Fennel contains antioxidants, antimicrobial components and anti-inflammatory volatile oils, as well as beta-carotene (which is converted to vitamin A in the body) and vitamin C, all of which play an important role in maintaining the health of mucus membranes that protect organs such as the respiratory tract.

FENUGREEK   Ancient Egyptians used fenugreek medicinally to ease congestion, brewing the seeds to make a tea, which can help to dissolve mucus in your lungs, throat and sinuses.

GINGER   Ginger contains minerals such as magnesium, chromium and zinc, which can help improve circulation, thus keeping extremities warm in the winter. Consuming ginger can also help to increase body temperature.

HORSERADISH   The punchy oils released when a horseradish root is cut have been shown to possess strong antibacterial properties. The root can also help circulation and clear congestion.

LAVENDER   In winter, I embrace the silvery, rosemary-like leaves of lavender, which are as relaxing as the summery purple flowerheads. Both have anti-inflammatory properties and are brilliant for relaxing the mind and helping ease the body into restful sleep.

NUTMEG   This spice helps stimulate the release of serotonin, which creates feelings of relaxation. The lacy coating of a nutmeg, mace, has similar medicinal qualities and flavours.

OREGANO   This woody herb has a warming flavour as well as thermogenic properties that can help increase circulation. Additionally, it's one of the best herbs to help the body fight bad bacteria and has carvacrol and thymol compounds, which can protect against some viruses.

PEPPER   Black pepper is a winter wonder spice that improves digestion, helps the body get rid of toxins, aids circulation and increases body heat during the cold months. It contains a potent antioxidant called piperine, which helps increase the absorption of selenium, B vitamins and beta-carotene.

ROSEMARY   An unsung circulatory support herb with similar properties to turmeric and ginger. It can help ease inflammation and increase blood flow to the brain, thus assisting with memory.

SAGE   All the woody, winter-surviving herbs are brilliant for suppressing bad bacteria and soothing mucosal membranes, which help calm sore throats and painful coughs. Like rosemary, sage also supports brain health, which is perhaps why a wise person is often called a 'sage'.

STAR ANISE   In traditional Chinese medicine, star anise is steeped in water to make a tea, which is then used to treat respiratory infections.

SZECHUAN PEPPER   This zingy, citrusy spice is high in antioxidants and helps to stimulate both the digestion and the circulation.

THYME   The go-to herb if you have a sore throat. Its active ingredient, thymol, has antiseptic, antifungal and antibacterial properties, which help soothe and heal inflamed throats.

TURMERIC   A thermogenic winter warmer, turmeric is a potent spice that can help the body eliminate bacterial infection. It's also anti-inflammatory and can ease the pain caused by several ailments, including soothing sore throats.

WINTER FIVE SPICE

There's depth to the casual sobriquet 'warming' attached to so many spices. Ginger, chilli and black pepper are a few that instantly make you feel toasty. Some spices, such as those used in the recipe below, can actually increase heat in the digestive system and throughout the body. This blend is the base of a delicious curry powder.

I love it paired with roasted parsnips finished with Mayan pepita pesto (see page 218), rubbed on lamb shoulder, or dusted over roasted sweet potatoes.

MAKES 75G (5 TBSP)

2 tbsp cumin seeds
1 tbsp black peppercorns
2 tsp cardamom pods and/or 1 cinnamon stick
1 tbsp ground turmeric
½ tsp cayenne pepper, or less for a milder blend

You can use pre-ground spices but, for more depth of flavour, dry-roast the whole spices and then grind them, once cooled, in a spice (or coffee) grinder. Store in a lidded jar for up to 1 year.

To dry-roast, set a large frying pan over a medium heat. Add the cumin seeds, peppercorns, crushed cardamom pods (you can leave the skins on as it adds extra flavour) and/or cinnamon stick. Once toasted, cool, then grind to a powder and mix in the turmeric and cayenne pepper.

MASALA CHAI

The foundations of the famous drink made with this spice blend were laid some five thousand years ago. According to legend, an Indian emperor combined the now-iconic medley of warm spices to make a drink to be sipped during the business of court, in order to remain alert. Historically, the chai was caffeine-free and used in Ayurvedic medicine for its warming properties.

The composition of sweet, aromatic spices is very similar to those used in winter baked goods such as Swedish *pepparkakor*, English Christmas pudding and American pumpkin pie. So beyond its use as the base for a warming drink (I like brewing mine with rooibos and oat milk), this is delicious in all manner of winter bakes and equally lovely lending subtle sweetness to savoury dishes. I've suggested its use throughout the book, such as in Spiced figgy jam and Golden carrot cake (see pages 44 and 252).

MAKES 50G (10 TSP)

2 cinnamon sticks, or 1 tbsp ground cinnamon
1 tsp whole cardamom pods, or ½ tsp ground cardamom seeds
1 tsp black peppercorns, or ½ tsp freshly ground black pepper
1 tsp whole cloves, or ½ tsp ground cloves
2 whole star anise, or ¼ tsp ground star anise

You can use pre-ground spices, but for more depth of flavour, try dry-roasting whole spices (see opposite) and then grind, once cooled, in a spice (or coffee) grinder. Store in a lidded jar for up to 1 year.

For a delicious chai, warm 250ml milk of your choice with 1 tbsp tea leaves or a teabag (I love using rooibos, which has a similar strength and depth to black tea, but is naturally caffeine-free).

Once your tea is strongly brewed, whisk in 1 tsp Masala chai.

SWEET

THINGS

The word 'treat' is poetically pliant, especially in relation to food. It can reference indulgence and pampering, as well as healing and nurture, and they can all beautifully intertwine.

We need to take time to look after ourselves. Luckily, we can tickle our taste buds and spike our neurotransmitters while also strengthening our immune systems with nourishment... and thus, along the way, eradicate the concept of 'guilty pleasures'. Those are two words I'll happily untangle.

This chapter is about having your cake and eating it too. I've had delicious creative fun in the kitchen swapping refined sugar for honey, dates and maple syrup, ingredients we sought when our ancestral sweet tooth beckoned.

A NATURALLY SWEET TRIPTYCH

Ancient Egyptians sought wild honey from treetop bees' nests ten thousand years ago, both for its decadent sweetness and for its medicinal qualities. Raw local honey is rich with benefits. Though it still can spike our blood sugar, it's a valuable source of trace minerals and nutrients – unlike cane sugar – and it has antibacterial properties that are just what we need to fight off winter bugs.

The chewy caramel notes and brown sugar-like texture of dates are also a brilliant refined-sugar swap. Dates are one of the oldest cultivated fruits in the world and are packed with antioxidants, fibre, vitamins such as B6 and minerals: they contain more potassium weight-for-weight than a banana. While, yes, dates are a concentrated source of sugar, their high fibre content helps balance that out, plus they have a lower glycaemic level than refined sugar, which prevents such a drastic blood-sugar spike while also feeding the good bacteria in the gut.

Maple syrup is an equally alluring refined-sugar swap. Not only does it have more iron, calcium, zinc and potassium than honey, but it's also a brilliant plant-based alternative.

*What good is the warmth of summer
without the cold of winter to give it sweetness?*

ROASTED RHUBARB CRANACHAN

I'm taking lots of liberties here. Cranachan is a traditional Scottish dessert made with whisky-sweetened cream, raspberries and oats.

My primary motivation in cooking is seasonality. Rhubarb (albeit indoor grown) is pretty much the only fruit – I know, technically it's a veg – you can harvest in the UK in January. It offers a similar sweet sharpness and blushing hue to that of raspberries and is delicious with oats and a creamy base. I've opted for yogurt or kefir in place of cream, and a rose water swap for whisky, but veer more towards the classic if you prefer. I love this pairing and make versions of it throughout the year, using different fruits roasted to concentrate their natural sugars. Tea makes a brilliant swap for orange or clementine juice: apple slices roasted in chamomile tea are a delicious variation.

SERVES 4

4 large rhubarb stalks, or 8–12 smaller stalks (total weight 800g–1kg)
2 large blood oranges, or navel oranges, or 4 clementines
1 tbsp rose water (optional)
2 tbsp honey, or maple syrup
100g rolled oats, or buckwheat groats
1 tsp ground cardamom and/or ground cinnamon
4 tbsp seeds and/or nuts
500g Greek yogurt, or Kefir labneh (see page 256)

Preheat the oven to 180°C/170°C fan. Cut the rhubarb into 3–4cm pieces at a slight angle, giving elongated points to each end.

Arrange the rhubarb in a baking dish: ideally you want it nestled in a single layer and not overcrowded, or it will steam rather than roast, but it shouldn't be too spaced apart or it will dry out. Finely grate a dusting of orange or clementine zest over the top (about 1 tsp). Squeeze over enough of the juice to come about halfway up the rhubarb: you want it moistened, but not swimming in juice.

Place the rhubarb in the centre of the oven and roast for 30 minutes until most (if not all) the juice has been absorbed and the rhubarb is tender and lightly coloured at the edges. Add the rose water, if using, and honey or maple syrup and set aside to cool.

Place the oats or buckwheat groats, spice(s) and seeds or nuts in a frying pan set over a medium heat and lightly toast them, just until they pick up a hint of colour.

Spoon the rhubarb and some of its honeyed juices into bowls, water tumblers or wine glasses. Cap with a generous spoonful of yogurt or labneh. Finish with the spiced, seeded or nutty oats or groats.

GINGER BISCUITS

In Sweden, 13 December is known as *Luciadagen* (Lucia's Day), but as it's so close to the winter solstice, there are echoes of earlier, more pagan celebrations lurking beneath the Christian moniker and they are focused around the return of light, albeit a few days early. 'Lucia' comes from the Latin word *lux*, after all, which means 'light'. In the Christian era, Lucia thus became the symbol of the return of the Sun out of the darkness.

Saffron buns and ginger biscuits such as these, known as *pepparkakor*, are eaten as part of the celebration. Historically they contained pepper as a boost to the other warming spices, though that has largely been lost over time and isn't included in most modern recipes. I've returned it to the mix, as well as lightening the recipe by using dates in place of honey. You can keep a log of this cookie dough in the freezer, slice and bake it from frozen, allowing two or three more minutes to cook.

MAKES ABOUT 16

65ml olive oil, plus more for the tray
75g buckwheat flour, plus more (optional) to dust
1 tbsp ground cinnamon
½ tsp ground cloves
good twist of black pepper (optional)
1 tsp baking powder
pinch of sea salt
150g pitted dates, finely chopped
2 tbsp finely grated root ginger

Preheat the oven to 180°C/170°C fan. Rub a little oil over a baking tray.

Place the buckwheat flour, ground spices, baking powder and sea salt in a large bowl and mix thoroughly: using a whisk helps. Add the dates, ginger and olive oil and blend until you have a soft, workable dough. It might seem a little oily: if you feel it's too much so, dust a little flour over.

Shape the dough into a log 3cm in diameter. Chill for 30 minutes in the refrigerator, or 10 minutes in the freezer to firm up. Cut the dough log into 5mm-thick rounds for bite-sized biscuits. (For larger biscuits, scoop the dough into 1 tbsp rounds instead.)

Arrange on a baking tray with a little space around each biscuit. (You may need to bake these in 2 batches.) Bake in the centre of the oven for 8 minutes, or until just starting to darken and firm up around the edges.

They'll be quite soft as soon as you take them out of the oven, but will firm up as they cool, so leave them for 10 minutes before transferring to a wire rack. They will keep in an airtight container for up to 1 week.

*'The night treads heavily
around yards and dwellings
In places unreached by sun
the shadows brood.
Into our dark house she comes
bearing lighted candles,
Saint Lucia, Saint Lucia.'*

Y

A traditional Saint Lucia Day carol
sung in Sweden

LEMON SNOWBALLS

This recipe is dedicated to my granny, Ima Mae. One of her favourite treats was a lemon-flavoured wafer bar: she used to pick me up from school and we'd share one when we got to her house. She also loved coconut and would have adored these light, lemony biscuits bound by the natural sweetness of coconut, with an added touch of maple syrup to make them more indulgent. To store these and bake when you want them, you can shape the mixture into a log, then freeze. The dough log can be cut and cooked from frozen (allow two or three more minutes in the oven).

MAKES 12

1 egg white, or 1 tbsp ground flaxseed
pinch of sea salt (optional)
1 tbsp water (optional)
75g coconut oil
4 tbsp maple syrup
100g desiccated coconut
100g ground almonds
finely grated zest of 1 lemon, plus 2 tbsp lemon juice

Preheat the oven to 180°C/170°C fan.

Whisk the egg white with a pinch of sea salt until light, frothy and white like a meringue. If using ground flax, mix it with 1 tbsp water.

Blend the remaining ingredients together in a separate bowl.

Fold the whipped egg white, or hydrated ground flaxseed, into the lemon mixture.

Spoon 1 tsp rounds of the mixture on to a baking sheet. Bake in the centre of the oven for 7–10 minutes or until just golden and set.

The biscuits will keep in an airtight container for up to 1 week.

PARIS TAHINI BISCUITS

I've always loved Paris and I seem to mostly visit the city in winter. In fact, often in February, around the time my birthday falls. After a relatively recent visit, I returned home a little sad to have left, but cheered by a plate of sesame-kissed tahini biscuits made by my friend Sara. She is one of the most giving humans on the planet and these wonderful biscuits are just one of the many treats I came home to when she lived with us. I crave them all the time. Sara didn't remember where she'd found the recipe, so I made up my own using a peanut butter cookie recipe (an American childhood favourite) as the base and swapping out its nutrient-lacking refined sugars for equally delicious but more nourishing sweeteners. Every time I make these, I think of Paris in February and my lovely friend Sara.

Do be tempted to scale up the recipe, if you like, to make a log of dough you can freeze, then slice, coat with sesame seeds and cook from frozen (allow two or three more minutes in the oven), for instant cookie satisfaction another time.

MAKES ABOUT 16

100g maple syrup
100g tahini
2 tbsp olive oil
½ tsp ground cinnamon
½ tsp baking powder
100g ground almonds
3–4 tbsp sesame seeds
pinch of sea salt (oak-smoked salt is lovely here)

Preheat the oven to 180°C/170°C fan.

Whisk the maple syrup and tahini together with the oil, cinnamon and baking powder. Fold in the ground almonds and use your hands or a spoon to bring the mixture together into a relatively stiff but workable dough.

Scoop the dough into teaspoon-sized balls. Roll the balls in the sesame seeds, then flatten them into 1cm-thick rounds. Transfer the rounds to baking sheets, arranging them so they're about 3cm apart. (These don't stick, so there's no need to line the baking sheets.) Sprinkle with sea salt.

Bake the cookies for about 8 minutes, until the bottoms are golden. They can be stored for up to 1 week in an airtight container, though they will become softer over time.

CHOCOLATE CHAGA HALVA

There's a lot of alchemy in these little morsels; your hands will turn the 'base metal' of the mixture into gold. When you mix honey and tahini together, it seizes up and becomes coarse and grainy, which is not what you want in halva. So the magic ingredient for this recipe, beyond the addition of a mushroom elixir, is your hands. Massage the concentrated tahini-honey nectar and it transforms into a silky fudge of sorts.

Adding *chaga* mushroom powder to the mix is an optional but wonderful health-boosting addition. The mushrooms have been used for centuries in Siberia and Asia to support the immune system. Their flavour complements the cacao or cocoa powder, lending a richer, more sophisticated taste without being too obvious, odd or overpowering.

MAKES 12–16 PIECES

100g dark tahini
2 tbsp raw cacao powder, or cocoa powder
2 tsp *chaga* (see page 278), or any powdered mushroom blend
1 tbsp honey, or maple syrup
1 tsp ground cinnamon (optional)
pinch of sea salt (I love oak-smoked salt here)
½ tsp sesame seeds (optional)

Give the tahini a good stir before measuring it. Mix all the ingredients apart from the sesame seeds together until you have a grainy paste.

Knead the mixture with your hands until it turns into a smooth, fudge-like dough (see recipe introduction).

Press into a small container (16 × 12cm is enough for this). The tin doesn't have to be lined, as there's enough oil in the tahini to prevent it from sticking, though lining it will help you to lift the halva out once it has set. I like this mixture to lie about 1cm deep, so when you cut it, each piece is about 1 tsp. Smooth the top. Dust the sesame seeds, if using, over, then set in the refrigerator for 10 minutes to firm up before cutting. It will store in an airtight container in the refrigerator for up to 1 month.

FORAGED FLORENTINES

This recipe is dedicated to my partner Stewart, as the first time I ever made florentines was for his birthday (they are one of his favourite sweets). I love them, too. Most shop-bought versions contain copious amounts of sugar, as well as more processed glucose syrups. I gave them a lighter touch on my initial attempt and have been refining my recipe ever since.

Adding orange juice to maple syrup to make the binding caramel works so beautifully and I love the sharp contrast of a hint of wild hedgerow fruits in the mix, too, but you can go with more classic dried fruits if that's what you have to hand. My first batch featured dried sour cherries which I'd foraged from a tree on my street, but come winter, I like to use dried elderberries in the mix (buy them online or in some health food shops if you haven't squirrelled away your own). You can also add a hint of rosehip powder, or fresh or dried apple peel, to boost both flavour and vitamin C.

MAKES ABOUT 12

2 tbsp ghee (for homemade, see page 214), or coconut oil
25g pitted dates
2 tbsp maple syrup
1 clementine, or ½ orange (you will need 1 tsp finely grated citrus zest plus 3 tbsp juice)
1 tsp buckwheat flour, or any flour
3 tbsp dried fruit (try mixing chopped apricots, slivers of chopped mango, sour cherries, dried elderberries, rosehip and/or hawthorn berry powder)
3 tbsp nuts and/or seeds
pinch of sea salt
90g dark chocolate

Optional extras
hint of your favourite spice (cardamom, mixed spice, finely grated root ginger)
rose water, or orange blossom water
edible rose petals, chopped

Preheat the oven to 180°C/170°C fan.

Place the ghee or coconut oil in a saucepan. Finely chop the dates and add them with the maple syrup, citrus zest and juice. Warm over a medium heat, mashing the dates with the back of a spoon to help them dissolve.

Once it has thickened a little, fold in the flour, then the dried fruits, nuts and/or seeds. Add the salt. Gently cook the mixture for 1 minute, stirring all the time until it starts to come together and adding any optional extras you want.

I normally try to avoid greaseproof paper, but it's needed here: line a baking tray with greaseproof paper, or reusable baking liners or muffin cups (the latter

help give perfect rounds). Spoon 1 tsp of the caramel-bound dried fruit and nut/seed mixture on the paper or liner or into the muffin cups. Flatten each dollop into a small round and tidy up the edges. Bake on the top oven shelf for 5–7 minutes to further caramelise the ingredients together. Remove from the oven and tidy the edges of each biscuit further, if needed. Allow to cool fully.

Finely chop the chocolate and put it in a heatproof bowl set over a pan holding a shallow pool of simmering water (don't let the bowl touch the water). Let it melt slowly and don't stir until most of it has melted.

Flip each biscuit over and coat the flat, bottom side of each with chocolate. Flash the biscuits in the freezer or refrigerator to help the chocolate set. Once set, you can eat them straight away, or store in the refrigerator or at room temperature for up to 2 weeks. They also freeze beautifully and can almost be eaten from frozen (depending on your teeth!) or defrosted at room temperature for around 1 hour.

HONEYED APPLE CAKE

This is one of my favourite apple cake recipes, inspired by Dorset apple cake, but reinvented to replace the sugar with dried fruit and feature honey as a sweet, sticky, golden gloss on top. It makes me think about the walk down the track at River Cottage. As you venture down to the farmhouse, past the gorse-edged woodland, you pass the apiary, also framed by gorse. In winter, those spiky shrubs are the only splash of colour around, with their yellow petals providing cheer while the bees cluster inside their hives to keep warm. On the opposite side of the track is one of the farm's orchards, with its skeletal trees looking like characters in a Tim Burton Christmas film. In winter, the farm normally still has a store of honey from the hives and apples from the orchard, which marry together in perfect harmony in this cake.

SERVES 8–12

200ml olive oil, plus more for the tin
3 large eggs
200g kefir, or natural yogurt (Greek-style is fine)
200g pitted dates, dried figs, or dried apricots
1 tbsp baking powder
1 tbsp Masala chai (see page 231), mixed spice, or ground cinnamon
pinch of sea salt
3 apples, coarsely grated, plus 1–2 (optional), finely sliced
100g spelt flour, or buckwheat flour
150g ground almonds
handful of flaked almonds (optional)
2–3 tbsp honey

Preheat the oven to 160°C/150°C fan. Lightly oil a 20–23cm cake tin, ideally with a removable base.

Using a blender or food processor, blend the olive oil, eggs, kefir or yogurt, dates or other dried fruits, baking powder, spice and salt together to a smooth purée.

Put the purée in a large bowl. Fold in the grated apples, then carefully fold in the flour and almonds. Transfer the mixture to the prepared tin, gently levelling the surface. For an added flourish, you can arrange fine slices of apple over the top (I leave skins on) or scatter with a generous handful of flaked almonds for crunch.

Bake in the centre of the oven for about 1 hour until golden and set in the middle. To test, insert a skewer or small knife into the middle of the cake; if it comes out clean, the apple cake is cooked.

Place the tin on a wire rack and leave until completely cold before removing from the tin. Drizzle the honey over to glaze, then serve.

MAPLE GINGER PEARS

As the temperatures in Canada start to climb just above the freezing mark, the 'sugaring' period in the maple woods begins. 'Sugaring' is a term coined by the Anishinaabe, from the Great Lakes region of Canada. They were the first to harvest the rising sap from maple trees as the weather swings from winter to spring, a local source of delicious sweetness before imports of cane sugar arrived. The rising thermometer is what causes the sap, stirred from the tree's winter stores, to circulate.

Holes are strategically drilled into the trunks and, on good years, a single tap hole can yield up to three hundred and sixty-four litres of maple sap. However, 98 per cent of this raw sap is water. Boiled down, the two per cent of sugar in such a yield will only equate to two litres of amber nectar, which is why maple syrup is precious stuff. I've used it modestly here, partnered with the intensified natural sugars in pears.

SERVES 4

4 pears
8 fresh bay leaves
4 thin slices of root ginger
2 tbsp maple syrup

Preheat the oven to 200°C/190°C fan.

Halve the pears and cut out the cores, but leave the skins on. Nestle the halved pears in a baking dish, cut sides down, tucking a bay leaf under each half.

Slide into the oven and roast for 30 minutes, or until the pears are still holding their shape but are very tender and have a toffee-like edge.

While they cook, cut the ginger slices into fine julienne strips. Remove the baking dish from the oven after the 30 minutes is up and flip the pears over, so they lie cut sides up. Scatter the ginger over the pears and drizzle the maple syrup over, too. Return to the oven for 15–20 minutes or until you can see that the cut sides of the pears have a kiss of caramelised gold.

Serve warm or cold. These are delicious paired with kefir or yogurt, or, for a more substantial dessert, serve alongside Ginger biscuits or Paris tahini biscuits (see pages 240 and 244).

GOLDEN CARROT CAKE

You will never have eaten anything like this before, but it's delicious. It's packed with carrots, but miles away from the classic that usually bears this recipe title. The cake happily evolved when I had a glut of carrots from Tamarisk Farm in Dorset. Nassima – the brilliant photographer who brings winter's magic to life throughout this book – and I had gone to Tamarisk to take some photos. I bought a bag of wonky carrots from their farm shop.

Organic carrots have an intense sweetness, as all good carrots should, and I was curious to see if their natural sugars, married with the inherent sweetness of coconut, would be enough to produce a plausible cake. Needing only the help of a few dates, it works. The lack of refined sugar, which does provide structure in a cake, makes for a velvety, mousse-like texture, but that is no bad thing. I haven't served this to anyone who doesn't adore it.

SERVES 8

300g carrots
400ml can of coconut milk
6 pitted dates
thumb of root turmeric, finely grated, or 1 tsp ground turmeric
1 tbsp Masala chai (see page 231), or 1 tsp each ground cinnamon, cardamom and black pepper
1 tbsp baking powder
150g buckwheat flour, or brown rice flour
150g ground almonds
1 tsp coconut oil, or ghee (for homemade, see page 214), for the tin
2–3 tbsp salted almonds, flaked almonds, or ground almonds

Preheat the oven to 180°C/170°C fan.

Finely slice the carrots and simmer in a lidded pan with the coconut milk, dates, turmeric and chai or other spices for 20 minutes, stirring occasionally, until the carrots are tender right the way through. Purée the coconut carrot mixture until smooth and creamy. Fold through the baking powder, flour and ground almonds.

Brush a 900g loaf tin lightly with coconut oil or ghee. Spoon the batter into the tin, scatter with the salted almonds, flaked almonds or ground almonds and bake in the centre of the oven for 45 minutes, or until fully set in the centre (test with a toothpick or similar). The middle will crack a little and the cake should shrink from the sides.

Remove from the oven and let cool for at least 15 minutes before removing from the tin. Leave for a further 15 minutes to cool before you cut into it.

This is lovely served with a dollop of kefir, or Greek yogurt.

BANANA SPLIT

When I was a kid, I thought banana splits were healthy. You did get a whole portion of raw fruit, after all. I obviously turned a blind eye to the maraschino cherries and squirty cream… and all the rest. This is a playful twist on my childhood favourite, also reminiscent of summer campfires.

I used to take my son camping in Devon on an organic farm called Trill. The firepit there was where we gathered morning, lunch and night, some cooking over the dancing embers and all sharing stories of past and present. Chocolate-stuffed bananas were always served at some point.

While foil is often used to bake these, I've been roasting them in their skins, using those as a natural protective layer. It works a treat over the fire, while in the oven you get the added benefit of catching all the juices both from the skins and the fruit itself: as it cooks, the juices caramelise, offering a bonus caramel sauce to drizzle over the split!

FOR EACH PERSON

1 ripe banana
1 square of dark chocolate (12g)
2 tbsp dairy kefir, or plant-based kefir
2 tbsp double cream, or coconut cream
1 frozen and defrosted cherry, or cranberry, or rehydrate a dried fruit
   in a little juice or water
pinch of chopped nuts (optional)

Preheat the oven to 200°C/190°C fan.

Split the banana through the skin down the centre. Roughly chop the chocolate and tuck it into the seam, packing it in as deep as possible. Try to cover over the chocolate with the banana skin and flesh as much as you can, to protect it in the oven.

Nestle the stuffed banana into a baking dish. Roast on the top shelf of the oven for 45 minutes, or until the skin has fully blackened and the banana appears caramelised. The chocolate will be completely melted.

Whip the kefir and cream together until light and airy like whipped cream.

Place the banana in a bowl or on a dish. Top with the whipped kefir, cherry or cranberry and nuts, if using. Drizzle with the sweet juices from the baking dish and serve.

KEFIR LABNEH

Straining the whey from kefir or yogurt yields a small, mildly fermented fresh cheese that is rich in probiotics and completely delicious. If you strain it for long enough, it'll thicken until it can fully hold its shape. From there, you can spoon it into a cheese mould or basket to make it more like a cheese, or you can eat it more like a spreadable cream cheese. It's delicious in both sweet and savoury contexts. For the former, pair with honey and seasonal fruit, or use it as the base for a cheesecake. For a savoury treat, mix it with herbs and garlic to slather on oatcakes, Seedy crackers or a warm slice of Finnish emergency bread (see pages 41 and 20).

MAKES ABOUT 350G

500g natural cow's milk kefir, or goat's milk kefir, or natural yogurt
pinch of sea salt (optional)

Put the kefir or yogurt into a bowl and stir in the salt, if using (though it's optional, it does help draw the whey out more quickly). Line a sieve or colander with a clean tea towel or a double layer of muslin. Pour the kefir or yogurt into the cloth. Bring the sides of the cloth together and tie over the top to give you a kefir- or yogurt-filled parcel.

Hang the parcel over a bowl, suspending it with string, or more cloth, tied around the handle of a cupboard or similar (or just leave it in the sieve or colander over the bowl). Let it hang and drip for at least 6 hours, or up to 2 days. If leaving it for any longer, it's best to cover the bowl of collecting whey with muslin.

The longer you leave it to hang, the more whey you'll get and the thicker the cheese will be. Typically, you lose around one-third of the weight. The labneh is fermented, so it won't spoil at room temperature during this period.

You can simply unwrap the cloth from the cheese and serve as is. Or you can dust it with a little salt and, if you like, brush with a little olive oil, then wrap it up in fresh sweet chestnut or fig leaves, or even wild horseradish leaves (each have their own unique flavours, chestnut being the most neutral). Or you can age the cheese in the refrigerator for up to 1 week: sprinkle a dusting of salt over it and set it on a plate. It makes an impressive dinner party piece.

Kefir vs yogurt

The main difference between kefir and yogurt is the number of good bacteria. Kefir contains up to twenty-eight different strains of bacteria, whereas yogurt typically has just two or three, lactobacillus being the primary one. The more you can populate your gut with diversity – in the case of kefir, lots of different bacteria rather than just a few – the better. And kefir is available to buy almost everywhere these days.

Another distinguishing factor between the two is the texture. Kefir is thinner and often referred to as 'pouring yogurt'. Its increased bacteria population helps break down the lactose in the milk, which makes it more digestible, but looser in texture.

The other difference is in how they're made. For yogurt, milk is heated, cultures are added (either freeze-dried bacteria or a few spoons of live yogurt) and it's then kept warm for twelve to twenty-four hours to allow the bacteria to multiply and culture the milk.

Kefir is made with curd-like grains (they look like cottage cheese), which are added to milk at room temperature for twenty-four to forty-eight hours. This thickens the milk, but not as much as yogurt, and the result is a little tangier and sometimes mildly fizzy.

Both are delicious, but kefir has added health benefits.

It's also worth noting that there are products on the market labelled as 'kefir yogurt', which are something in between: they normally contain around fourteen different types of gut-friendly bacteria and are thicker than kefir but thinner than yogurt.

You can source kefir grains online to make your own from scratch. Alternatively, mix 500ml full-fat milk with 150ml kefir in a bottle and ferment it in the refrigerator for three days, during which time the bacteria in the kefir will break down the natural sugars in the milk (the lactose), increasing the beneficial bacteria and transforming the milk into kefir.

CRUMBS CRUMBLE

I met London-based artist David Vallade in my local bookshop, Bookseller Crow. David drew illustrations for the shop window and was working on a campaign with the local park, to help educate people about feeding the ducks. The messaging was that stale bread is not ideal food for our waddling, pond-dipping friends. In fact, so much bread sold today isn't great for us, either. That said, slowly risen sourdough made with local, organic flour (wheat is one of the most absorbent crops and so absorbs more pesticides) is rich with nutrients. A good sourdough loaf is worth celebrating – and not feeding to ducks! – so this recipe was born. I love the depth of flavour the breadcrumbs bring and, if you're short of breadcrumbs, just swap them for more rolled oats or ground almonds.

SERVES 6–8

1kg apples (or swap up to 500g with other fruits such as rhubarb
   or pears)
1 tsp ground cardamom, or ground cinnamon, or Masala chai
   (see page 231)
6 tbsp maple syrup
1 tbsp ground cinnamon, or Masala chai (see page 231)
75g stale breadcrumbs
75g rolled oats
75g ground almonds
3–4 tbsp butter, ghee, coconut oil, or olive oil

Preheat the oven to 200°C/190°C fan.

Peel the apples (use the cores and peel for Apple scraps chai, see page 272) and chop into bite-sized pieces. If adding rhubarb or pears, you don't need to peel them and can just finely slice (though core the pears).

Pile the fruit into a large baking dish that will hold it in a fairly shallow layer. Dust the 1 tsp ground cardamom, cinnamon or chai over the fruit and stir through 2 tbsp of the maple syrup.

Slide into the oven for 45 minutes or until the fruit has collapsed into a near-compote texture.

Meanwhile, make the topping. Mix the 1 tbsp ground cinnamon or Masala chai with the breadcrumbs and whizz in a food processor or blender, to make them fine. Add the rolled oats and ground almonds. Fold in the remaining 4 tbsp maple syrup and work in enough butter, ghee or oil to bring the mixture together into just-moistened clumps.

Scatter it over the cooked fruit and return to the oven for 20 minutes, or until golden on top with sweet sticky juices bubbling around the sides. Delicious warm with a cool dollop of Greek yogurt or kefir.

CHOCOLATE, PEAR AND MISO MOUSSE

Cravings are spurred by the body's specific needs and, when it comes to chocolate, the stress-relieving magnesium it contains is often just what the doctor ordered. This dessert gives you a good dose of that, but without the sugar. In its place is raw pear, which will feed the good bacteria in your gut, as well as oil which will give your brain fuel. The recipe can easily be scaled down; I love whipping up a single batch to eat when I'm in need of a bit of chocolate indulgence. It's also delicious topped with lightly toasted nuts or seeds.

SERVES 4

4 large ripe pears, or 4 smaller ripe pears (total weight about 400g)
4 tbsp raw cacao powder, or cocoa powder
2 tbsp olive oil, or walnut oil
1–2 tbsp honey, or maple syrup
1–2 tsp miso
pinch of sea salt

Peel the pears and reserve some of the peelings, cutting them into fine wisps to decorate at the end. Cover and refrigerate until needed.

Use a teaspoon or small knife to carve the seeds out of the pears. Cut off the knobbly bases and the stalks at the top. Blend the prepared pears with the remaining ingredients until smooth and creamy, starting with 1 tbsp honey or maple syrup and 1 tsp miso and adding more, to taste, to reach your desired savoury-sweet balance.

Spoon into glasses or dishes and chill until ready to serve; it stores beautifully in the refrigerator for up to 3 days. Decorate with the reserved pear peelings.

STICKY CITRUS DATE CAKE

Inspired by an English comfort food classic, the mighty sticky toffee pud, this recipe amplifies the date element, yet melds and balances it with the sharp tang of winter citrus. Blood oranges are my favourite here, but in fact you can make this at any time of year, with whatever orange orbs you can lay your hands on. You can also grind up any nut you have or love in place of the almonds. (I once made this with freshly ground pecans and it was delicious.) And try playing around with different oils: next time I make it, I'm keen to try it with cobnut or hazelnut oil, along with ground hazelnuts.

This batter is also lovely baked in a muffin (or mini bundt) tin. Baked that way, it makes 8–12 muffins or mini bundts and you'll need to reduce the baking time to 18–20 minutes.

SERVES 8

75ml olive oil, plus more for the tin
200g pitted dates
2 tsp finely grated orange zest, plus 300ml freshly squeezed orange juice
    (see recipe introduction)
1 tsp bicarbonate of soda
thumb of root ginger, finely grated
1 tsp mixed spice
100g buckwheat flour
75g ground almonds, hazelnuts, pecans, or walnuts
pinch of sea salt

For the sticky topping
300ml freshly squeezed orange juice

Preheat the oven to 180°C/170°C fan. Lightly oil a 900g loaf tin.

Chop the dates in half, put them in a small saucepan and cover with the orange zest and juice. Simmer gently for 5 minutes until the dates are soft.

Take off the heat and stir in the bicarbonate of soda, which will froth as you add it. Blend the juicy bicarb dates until smooth with the ginger and mixed spice.

Fold in the buckwheat flour and ground nuts, the 75ml olive oil and the pinch of salt.

Spoon into the prepared tin. Bake in the centre of the oven for 35 minutes, or until cooked and the sponge bounces back when pressed.

Meanwhile, gently boil the juice for the topping until it has reduced by half. Serve it warm in a jug alongside the cake, to pour over each slice.

ROASTED SQUASH MOUSSE

I've whipped the flavours of an American pumpkin pie into an indulgent mousse. It has all the depth of a creamy baked custard, but with minimal effort. Even better, it's rich in both probiotics (they add more good bacteria to your microbiome) and prebiotics (food for those bacterial 'pets' that keep your body happy and healthy).

SERVES 4

1 small squash, or ½ larger squash, total weight about 500g (butternut, Crown Prince, kabocha or onion squash all work a treat)
2 tsp mixed spice, or Masala chai (see page 231), or more as needed
1–2 × 1cm-thick slices of root ginger, to taste, or more as needed
10–12 pitted dates, or more as needed
up to 250g dairy kefir, or a plant-based alternative such as coconut kefir, or cashew kefir

To serve (optional)
dairy kefir, plant-based kefir, or Greek yogurt
toasted oats, nut, seeds and/or granola
Masala chai (see page 231)

Preheat the oven to 200°C/190°C fan.

Halve the squash. Scoop out the seeds (you can toast these to use for the topping). Place the squash halves on a baking sheet, cut side down. Roast in the oven for about 45 minutes, or until tender and caramelised around the edges. Set aside to cool down a bit.

Scoop out the squash flesh from the skin and place in a blender or food processor. Add the mixed spice or Masala chai, ginger, dates and half the kefir. Blitz until creamy and smooth, adding more kefir as needed.

Taste and add more spices or dates, if you like.

Pop in the refrigerator to chill for a few hours, then spoon into glasses and add your favourite toppings, such as a dollop more kefir or Greek yogurt and a finishing scatter of toasted oats, nuts, seeds and/or granola, or Masala chai, or all of them!

TONICS,

TEAS

AND
MOCKTAILS

To paraphrase Emily Dickinson:
winter is a delicious season to
drink in the 'liquor never brewed'.

Even on the shortest days, with the coldest nights, woodlands wink with tantalising treats. The citrusy brush of pine and the eye-catching rosy rouge of hawthorn can be transformed into brews straight from nature's apothecary. Tucked under the white blanket of frosty meadows hide equally delicious treats, such as dandelion roots, which taste like coffee yet help you ease into a delicious sleep. After drunken bees take flight, tipsy with the nectar of ivy and gorse, they cluster in the hive to stay warm and feast on their stores. If we're lucky, they'll have cellared extra honey for us to enjoy through winter, in toddies and more. The best tonics are on the house, courtesy of nature.

WINTER'S MIXOLOGIST

Stirred through the season are libations sparked by the riches of the wild. Harvested from far afield in Mexico, stored summer hibiscus blooms are married with the perfume of warming spices and the zing of winter citrus to create a steamy cauldron of sippable celebration. Wise oaks may have shed their leaves, but seductive notes from their toasted wood can be used to infuse tipples with an essence of vanilla that also brings a lift of cold-battling goodness.

In the spirit of indulgence – as deprivation is a hard master, most especially when it's cold outside – you can most certainly add a dash of whisky, a drop of wine or a thimble of rum to any of the recipes that follow. But if you want purer hydration, the drinks here are just what the doctor ordered.

*Winter is the perfect time
to raise a glass to good health.*

APPLE SCRAPS CHAI

The secret to perfect chai is to wholly extract the warming virtues of the spices. So give them a vigorous bash and let them infuse for a generous 15 minutes, or longer. Allowing the spices a brief spell to work their magic will also give the apple cores and peels time to release gut-soothing pectin, which lends the chai more body and flavour.

SERVES 2

cores and peels from 1–2 apples
pinch of saffron threads (optional)
large thumb of root ginger
1 cinnamon stick, or 1 tsp ground cinnamon
2 star anise
10 cardamom pods
10 cloves
10 black peppercorns
750ml water
1–2 tbsp honey, or to taste

Place the apple cores and peels in a medium-sized saucepan. Bash all the spices in a mortar and pestle, or on a board with a rolling pin or the base of a jam jar. You want to crush the ginger and release all the natural oils in the other spices. Add the spices to the saucepan with the measured water and simmer for 15 minutes (or longer) to extract as much flavour from the spices as possible.

Strain into teacups and sweeten to taste with the honey. Serve warm, keeping any extras in the refrigerator to reheat later.

GOJI GINGER TEA

Sweet and blushing in colour with a smoky, tea-like flavour, goji berries can be steeped into a delicious brew, a practice embraced by practitioners of traditional Chinese medicine for centuries. Known as wolfberries or *gŏu qĭ* in China, the dense dried fruits are brilliant for supporting liver and kidney function: the organs that help our bodies rid themselves of toxins.

Goji berries are also the only food known to stimulate human growth hormones (HGH), which sound like steroids but aren't! These hormones actually help maintain youthful energy and vigour. In the Ningxia Hui region of Northern China, where goji berries are grown and eaten daily, there are sixteen times as many centenarians as there are in the rest of the country.

SERVES 1

1 tbsp dried goji berries
2 slices of root ginger
2 red dates or jujubes (optional)
250ml freshly boiled water

Place the goji berries, ginger and dates, if using, in a saucepan or teapot. Pour the measured boiling water over the top.

Simmer or steep for 10 minutes (simmering will draw out the flavours more), then strain and sip.

CHRISTMAS TREE TEA

On a frigid winter in 1536, the crew of French maritime explorer Jacques Cartier arrived in the village of Stadacona (now Québec City, Canada). The sailors were suffering from scurvy after their long voyage, and it's said a native man brewed a pot of pine needle tea, which had a rapid curative effect.

Pine needle tea has four to five times more vitamin C than orange juice, or a lemon. Brewing the needles – which releases a gentle fragrance of vanilla married with sharp citrusy notes – produces a drink that's great for easing congestion, which is why the first nation Haudenosaunee (commonly known as Iroquois) embraced pine's resplendent health benefits.

If you want to use a sprig of your own Christmas tree, make sure it is organic and has not been treated with chemicals. (See overleaf for a guide to foraging for pine.)

SERVES 1

1 tbsp pine needles, or 1 large pine, spruce or fir sprig
1 dried or fresh strip of orange zest
2 cloves and/or ½ cinnamon stick
1 star anise (optional)
250ml freshly boiled water

Place all the ingredients apart from the measured water in a saucepan, or in a teapot.

Pour the measured boiling water over and – if using a saucepan – simmer over a very gentle heat so you don't destroy the nutrients or flavour, or steep in a teapot, for 10–15 minutes. (Simmering will draw out the flavours more.)

Strain and sip while steamy.

Foraging for pine

White pine is often the favoured conifer for culinary use, but you can open your world up to other organic or wild species, including Douglas firs, blue spruce and Scot's pine. One of the key identifying characteristics is the intense citrus aromatics of edible conifers. Yew needles, which are poisonous, are pretty much odourless. But you can avoid yew by looking at the back of their needles: yew needles are a drab green, whereas firs – which are safe to eat – have a silvery underside with a line down the centre.

DELICIOUS EDIBLE CONIFER SPECIES

Blue spruce (aka Colorado blue spruce)
Douglas fir
Noble fir
Norway spruce
Scots pine
Sitka spruce
White pine

SPECIES TO AVOID

Common juniper
Common yew
Lodge pole pine (aka shore pine)
Monterey cypress (aka macrocarpa)
Norfolk pine (aka Australian pine)
Ponderosa pine (aka blackjack, western yellow,
    yellow and bull pine)

If in doubt, seek advice from a plant expert or local forager, or source edible pine needles online.

Guide to medicinal mushrooms

CHAGA   For centuries, *chaga* has been used as a traditional medicine in Russia and other Northern European countries, mainly to boost immunity and overall health. *Chaga*'s magic trick is stimulating white blood cells, essential for fighting off harmful bacteria or viruses. Flavour-wise, it has a deep chocolate-meets-cinnamon taste with bitter mushroom notes.

LION'S MANE   These are large, white and shaggy with a lion's mane-like appearance. Research points to their ability to protect against dementia, reduce mild symptoms of anxiety and depression and help repair nerve damage (see page 302). The flavour is wholly unique, mimicking shellfish such as scallops, crab and lobster.

REISHI   This mushroom is said to improve the function of adrenal glands by working on the hypothalamus-pituitary-adrenal gland axis, calming the mind, easing anxiety and promoting sleep. It offers bitter flavour notes with hints of chocolate.

SHIITAKE   Typically grown on the decaying wood of deciduous trees (commonly the *shii* tree in Japan, hence its etymology, but chestnut, oak and maple are also used). It contains polysaccharides, which boost white blood cell production for fighting off microbes. The flavour is earthy, with a miso-like umami depth.

MUSHROOM MARY

The motivation to opt for a Bloody Mary as a hair of the dog, a concept approved by Hippocrates and written into classic Greek literature, is substantiated by the recipe's medicinal alchemy. Tomato juice alone is a rich source of rehydrating electrolytes and lycopene, which helps combat toxins in the liver. Add a vitamin C-rich hit of lemon zest and juice and a hint of immune-boosting and circulation-stimulating kimchi brine (a probiotic swap for Tabasco) and the benefits are boosted further.

I've long been a fan of pairing mushrooms with tomatoes as they lend a rich umami depth and, here, they give your hair of the dog further power to bite back. With or without vodka – and hungover or not – this tipple will infuse you with renewed energy, while wildly pleasing your taste buds.

SERVES 1

250ml tomato juice
1 tbsp kimchi brine
1 tsp shiitake, reishi, lion's mane, or chaga mushroom powder
 (see opposite)
fine grating of lemon zest and 1 tbsp lemon juice
10 good cracks of freshly ground black pepper
½ tsp miso, or 1 tsp Goji berry purée (optional, see below)
pinch of celery seeds (optional)
1–2 vodka shots (optional)
small, leafy celery stick from a celery heart (optional), to serve

Shake all the ingredients in a cocktail shaker with ice, or blend and pour over ice. Delicious and visually pleasing served with a refreshing celery stick.

GOJI BERRY PURÉE

A brilliant booster for your Mushroom Mary, or even your Bloody Mary, this lends a hint of fruity sweetness and body. It freezes well in ice-cube trays and makes 100ml, or enough for 8 drinks. Just gently simmer 4 tbsp goji berries with 100ml water for 5 minutes, then blend to a purée.

OXYMEL BITTERS

An oxymel is an old-fashioned herbal remedy which has been around for centuries. In its most basic form, it is simply a mixture of honey with vinegar, which are both healing on their own, but adding herbs and spices amplifies the potency while also giving a wild depth of flavour. For this recipe, I've gone for a mix of the botanicals featured in traditional bitters, making this oxymel the ideal secret ingredient for making a medicinal mocktail. This really does need to be diluted by at least 75 per cent. I foolishly took a swig from the bottle once – just to see what it was like – and it took my breath away!

MAKES 750ML

750ml apple cider vinegar
50g honey
pared zest of 1 grapefruit
2 tbsp fresh sloes, dried sloes, rosehips and/or elderberries (optional)
2 tbsp juniper berries
1 tbsp allspice berries
1 tbsp coriander seeds
2 teaspoons black peppercorns, or pink peppercorns
4 star anise
4 bay leaves
1 rosemary sprig

Whisk the vinegar and honey together and pour into a 1 litre bottle. Tuck the grapefruit zest into the bottle, with all the other ingredients.

Secure the bottle with a lid or a cork. Give it a good shake and leave it to infuse for at least 1 week before using, or up to 3 months: the longer you leave it, the stronger it will become in flavour and potency. Strain before using. It will happily keep unrefrigerated for 1 year, due to the preservative effect of the vinegar base, but tastes nicer chilled.

WHAT TO DO WITH THE BITTERS

To serve, strain 2–3 tbsp into a glass with ice and top up with sparkling water, or use in place of Angostura or other bitters in your favourite cocktails. Or try in The Count's first negroni (see page 282). It's also lovely to shake 1 tbsp bitters with 100ml pomegranate juice and top up with 100ml sparkling water or kombucha.

THE COUNT'S FIRST NEGRONI

Negronis, to my mind, are the ultimate cocktail to celebrate the bitter sweetness of winter citrus. The classic recipe features gin paired with sweet vermouth and bitters, often Campari. One of the key flavourings of that drink is chinotto, a small citrus from the myrtle-leaved orange tree. The juice and zest of chinotto have a bitterness on a par with that of Seville orange or grapefruit. This mocktail embraces all those flavours and nods to the origins of negroni: legend has it that the original didn't feature gin at all and, instead, the cocktail first mixed in 1919 in Florence for the Count Negroni had a medicinal focus.

FOR EACH PERSON

1 grapefruit
1 tsp cranberry juice, or hibiscus flowers
1 tsp Oxymel bitters (see page 280, optional)
3 cardamom pods
½ tsp coriander seeds
1 tsp honey, or maple syrup
pinch of sea salt
50ml white grape juice, white wine, or unflavoured kombucha

Use a vegetable peeler to cut a strip of zest from the grapefruit. Arrange the peel in a chilled glass for serving.

Juice the grapefruit and place in a cocktail shaker or blender with the cranberry juice or hibiscus flowers and the bitters, if using. Lightly crush the cardamom pods and add them with the coriander seeds, honey or maple syrup and pinch of salt. Shake or blend to combine all the flavours and extract the essence from the spices.

Strain into the zest-filled glass. Add a touch of ice, if you wish, and top up with the grape juice, wine or kombucha.

MULLED HIBISCUS

My mother's favourite flower was hibiscus. I'll forever treasure her joy and astute observational skills as she monitored the fleeting unfurling of those taut spiral-bound buds into blowsy blooms resembling frilly-hemmed cha-cha skirts. But hibiscus flowers only last for a day. The petals then open further, tumbling to wilt into the soil. If they're caught in their moment of glory and dried, their deep blushing beauty and tangy flavour is preserved, along with the flower's rich immune-boosting properties.

In Mexico, dried hibiscus flowers are simmered with seasonal fruit and spices in *ponche Navideño*, a festive celebratory punch brewed for Christmas, very much akin to mulled wine. Infusing the lush burgundy flowers is the perfect visual swap for red wine, and, married with a drop of honey, the flavour works, too.

SERVES 4

4 tbsp dried hibiscus flowers
2 cinnamon sticks
4 star anise
1 tbsp cardamom pods, crushed
1 tsp cloves
2 clementines
1 litre freshly boiled water
1–2 tbsp honey, or maple syrup

Place the hibiscus flowers in a saucepan with all the spices. Squeeze in the juice from one of the clementines and slice the other clementine. Add the juice and clementine slices to the mixture, then pour in the measured boiling water and gently simmer for 15 minutes.

Sweeten with the honey or maple syrup, to taste. Ladle into glasses and serve warm.

HONEY-FERMENTED TODDY

Whack some of nature's finest flu-fighting ingredients into a jar and ferment them with honey and you've got a superpower potion to keep you armoured-up when lurgies try to invade. But beyond its health-giving properties, this is a delicious dance of ingredients to satisfy your taste buds.

The fermented take here harks back to the original hot toddy, which can be traced to India. A drink of fermented palm sap called *taddy* in Hindi was deemed to be medicinal and it inspired Irish-born physician Robert Bentley Todd, who included spices in a concoction which he prescribed to patients.

Once fermented, take a soothing 1–2 tsp a day to help strengthen your immune system. Or dilute it with cooled boiled water and sip as a tea: perfect for soothing sore throats. You can also eat the lemons, they're fabulous in salads, or with grilled fish.

MAKES 150G

100g honey
1 small lemon, or ½ larger lemon, cut into 1cm-thick slices
thumb of root ginger, finely sliced
thumb of root turmeric, finely sliced, or ¼ tsp ground turmeric
ground cinnamon
6 black peppercorns

Trickle a layer of honey into a sterilised jar (see page 188) of at least 200g capacity. Place a slice each of lemon, ginger and turmeric (or a pinch of ground turmeric) on the honey, sprinkle with a pinch of cinnamon and add a black peppercorn.

Top with another layer of honey and then continue to layer the ingredients in the jar until you've used everything up, or nearly reached the top of the jar. The ferment needs oxygen, so leave a bit of headspace; this also makes it easier to shake the mix together as it matures.

Secure the jar with a lid. Give it a shake every day or 2 to help keep the lemon and spices covered and mixed in with the honey and open the jar for a while afterwards, to enable the ferment to get extra oxygen.

Leave to ferment for at least 2 weeks and up to 3 months at room temperature, or up to 1 year in the refrigerator.

CHAMOMILE CHARDONNAY

I love the purity of this recipe and its ability to pass as a plausible white wine replacement when you can't, or don't want to, drink a glass of regular wine with dinner. This is great when you want something to drink that feels indulgent and has the acidity to complement food.

This combination of ingredients offers just the right balance of flavours and, as a happy accident, they're also rich immune-boosting substances. Oak chips are optional, but easy to source online, and they have been used medicinally throughout history to treat the common cold, sore throats and bronchitis. Interestingly, the high tannin content of certain wines is typically a result of ageing wine in oak barrels. It's the oak's tannin that lends both flavour and antibacterial properies.

Kefir grains can also be purchased online (see page 302) and are used to ferment the delicious brew below, resulting in a lot of gut-friendly, good bacteria-boosting benefits, as well as giving the drink a more rounded wine-like complexity.

MAKES 1 LITRE

1 litre freshly boiled water
4 chamomile tea bags, or 4 tbsp dried chamomile flowers
2 fresh pine, spruce, or fir sprigs, or 2 tbsp dried needles
strip of lemon zest (about ½ lemon)
2 tbsp oak wood chips, or 2 tbsp oak-smoked water (optional)
2 tbsp golden caster sugar
3 tbsp kefir grains

Pour the measured boiling water over the chamomile, pine and lemon zest in a large heatproof bowl.

If you're using oak, toast it gently in a frying pan set over medium-high heat. You can use fine wood chips which look like desiccated coconut, or larger chips that look like coconut chips. Toast until fragrant (you'll get hints of vanilla scent when it's ready) and lightly golden.

Tip the toasted oak, if using, straight in with the brewing tea. Allow to steep for 30 minutes, then strain into a sterilised 1.5-litre jar (see page 188). Stir in the sugar, then, when fully cool, add the kefir grains.

Cover with a cloth and let it ferment for 2 days at room temperature. Strain, bottle and chill before drinking. It will keep happily in the refrigerator for 1 week. Store the kefir grains in the refrigerator with just enough water to keep them hydrated; they can be reused. To keep them happy, dust a spoonful of sugar over them, as that's their food source.

POMEGRANATE BEAUJOLAIS

On a frosty January evening, I served this as a non-alcoholic offering to a group of us feasting together. I had been asked to help a nutritionist friend curate a week of health-focused menus for her client, who was recovering from breast cancer treatment. The last thing I wanted was for our evening meals to seem austere, so each night I tried out different wine replacements. This was the biggest hit, even among the most sceptical diners.

While fresh pomegranate juice is best, you can certainly swap it for bottled. The juice is often likened to the foresty, smoky notes of a good Beaujolais and vice versa, as the young Gamay grape wine – which is high acidity and low in tannins – is often likened to the winter-ripening bauble-like fruit. Even richer as a health offering, pomegranate juice is three times more potent in antioxidants than red wine and also contains a type of acid which has been shown to slow down the growth of cancer cells.

SERVES 1

juice of 1 pomegranate, or 200ml bottled pomegranate juice
2 sage leaves
1 star anise
pinch of ground cinnamon
7 allspice berries
7 black peppercorns

Place the pomegranate juice in a blender with the sage, star anise, cinnamon, allspice berries and peppercorns. Blend and strain into glasses, or decant into a bottle, and lightly chill before serving.

If you don't have a blender, simply bash all the ingredients in a mortar and pestle, or crush with the base of a sturdy glass on a chopping board, and place in a bottle with the pomegranate to infuse at room temperature for at least 30 minutes, or chill it in the refrigerator overnight.

KOMBUCHA COLA

This is a whimsical recipe that evolved from making a honey-fermented take on mince pie filling. On tasting, it had a subtle cola flavour, so I tried brewing it up as a kombucha and I think it really works. While I'm not partial to the classic American fizzy drink, I love this spin and drinking it at Christmas evokes the iconic 1950s advertising images of Father Christmas, making it fun and festive. Perhaps one to leave out with mince pies on Christmas Eve.

MAKES 1 LITRE

1 litre freshly boiled water
4 black or oolong teabags, or 4 tbsp loose leaf black tea, or oolong tea
1 quince, or apple
1 tbsp finely grated root ginger
1 tsp ground cinnamon, or 1 cinnamon stick
6 cloves
½ tsp mixed spice
dusting of freshly grated nutmeg
2 tbsp dates and/or currants
1 tsp finely grated orange zest, or 1 long strip of zest
1 tsp finely grated lemon zest, or 1 long strip of zest
75g organic molasses, or brown sugar, plus 1 tbsp
1 kombucha SCOBY

In a large heatproof bowl, at least 1.5 litres in capacity, pour the measured boiling water over the tea. Grate in the quince or apple, leaving the skin on as it lends gut-soothing pectin, body and flavour. Add the ginger, spices, dates and/or currants and citrus zests.

Cover with a clean cloth and let the fruity, spiced tea mixture steep for 1–2 hours to really infuse all the flavours. Strain once brewed and press through a sieve to extract as much flavour and liquid as possible.

Whisk in the 75g molasses or sugar and pour into a sterilised 1.5–2 litre jar (see page 188). Add the kombucha SCOBY and cover with a clean cloth.

Ferment at room temperature (ideally 18–22°C) for 10–14 days. Check after 1 week: the flavour should be somewhere in between a sweetened tea and apple cider vinegar. The longer you leave it, the sharper and more vinegary it will taste.

After the kombucha has brewed to your liking, strain it through muslin to remove any strands of SCOBY (aka 'SCOBY snot'!) which can be unpalatable.

Add the remaining 1 tbsp sugar to the brew and pour into a 1 litre sterilised bottle (see page 188). Leave at room temperature for 24 hours: the additional sugar will feed the live cultures in the bottled brew, which will help carbonate the drink, giving you a cola-like fizz. Chill for up to 1 week, or longer, though the flavour will start to become tangy and less cola-like.

CRANBERRY KOMBUCHA

There are so many fun flavours you can add to kombucha. This is a delicious festive ferment, rich with immune-boosting properties.

MAKES 1 LITRE

4 black or oolong teabags, or 4 tbsp loose leaf black tea, or oolong tea
1 litre freshly boiled water
75g organic molasses, or caster sugar, plus 2 tbsp
1 kombucha SCOBY
100ml cranberry juice
thumb of root ginger, juiced or finely sliced
4 cloves, freshly ground
4 tbsp oak wood chips (optional)

There are 2 stages to making this. First, you need to make a basic kombucha. To do this, brew the teabags or loose leaf tea in the measured boiling water. Let it steep for 1 hour, giving you a strong tea base that has cooled to room temperature.

Strain the teabags or leaves out. Whisk in the 75g molasses or sugar. Once it has dissolved, pour the sweetened tea into a sterilised 1.5–2 litre jar (see page 188) and add the SCOBY. Cover the jar with a clean cloth and leave at room temperature (ideally 18–22°C) for 1–2 weeks. Check after 1 week: the flavour should be somewhere in between a sweetened tea and apple cider vinegar. The longer you leave it, the sharper and more vinegary it will taste.

After the kombucha has brewed to your liking, strain it through muslin to remove any strands of SCOBY (aka 'SCOBY snot'!) which can be unpalatable.

Mix with the cranberry juice, the 2 tbsp sugar, ginger and cloves.

Set a frying pan over a high heat. Add the wood chips, if using, and toast for 1–2 minutes or until they smell a bit smoky and are lightly toasted. Make a 'teabag' for the wood chips using a piece of muslin or clean fabric. Secure with a piece of string, or simply tie the cloth securely. Add to the kombucha, cover with a cloth and let it steep with the wood chips for 8–12 hours.

Remove the wood chip teabag, if using. Pour the kombucha into a 1 litre sterilised bottle (see page 188) and secure with a lid. Leave at room temperature for 1–2 days, or until a bit of carbonation has built up in the drink (open it to see). Store in the refrigerator until ready to drink. It will keep for 2 weeks but it becomes progressively tangier over that time, as the sugars ferment out slowly each day.

NIGHT NOG

Egg nog has long been one of my favourite tipples at Christmas. It's basically like drinking cold custard. The classic mixture of cream, rum, sugar and egg yolk isn't necessarily a recipe for a good night's rest, but one of the most nostalgic features of a good nog is the generous dusting of nutmeg on top, which is perfect for easing you into a restful winter slumber. I've paired it with other sleep-easy ingredients such as banana and hemp, oats or almonds that emulate the creamy comfort of custard while offering a heady dose of nod-inducing tryptophan.

SERVES 2

500ml hemp milk, oat milk, or almond milk
1 tsp ground hemp seeds, flaxseed, or chia seeds (soaked if you like, see page 30)
1 banana, peeled (and frozen, if you want the drink to be chilled)
1 tsp *ashwagandha* powder (optional, see page 49)
1 tsp ground cinnamon
¼ tsp freshly ground nutmeg, plus more to serve
drop of honey, or maple syrup (optional)

Blend the milk, seeds, banana (try frozen, or add a few ice cubes for a thicker, creamier consistency), *ashwagandha*, cinnamon and nutmeg. Taste and whizz in the honey or maple syrup, if using, to taste.

Pour into glasses and finish with a decorative cap of nutmeg.

SPICED TAHINI COCOA

Comforting as a down-feather duvet, this drink is also stress-soothing. It's my go-to hot chocolate when I want something indulgent that's not going to spike my blood sugar, or leave me jittery. In fact, the careful blend of ingredients here has the opposite, calming effect.

The magnesium in cacao soothes the nervous system, while the Ayurvedic herb *brahmi* (easily sourced online, see page 302) provides a further mental-health benefit and lends an earthy, mushroomy-leaning undertone. But I've offered a few alternatives with similar effects. The Peruvian root *maca* is also brilliant for calming and focusing the mind but it has a more energising effect. The *chaga* is great if you want to give your cocoa a literal mushroom note that has immune-boosting benefits. Or opt for powdered beetroot (I make my own by drying clean, peeled beetroot skins in a low oven or at room temperature, which are easily powdered in a mortar and pestle or coffee grinder). The beetroot is great for circulation and heart health and it lends a red velvet tone – flavour-wise and visually – to the cocoa. (For more on booster powders, see pages 48–49.)

Any which way you go, this drink (pictured opposite) is the perfect cup of *hygge* to cheer you on dark, cold winter days.

SERVES 1

1 tbsp tahini
2–3 pitted dates
1½ tbsp raw cacao powder, or cocoa powder
1 tsp *brahmi*, *maca*, *chaga*, or beetroot powder (optional, see pages 49,
    278 and recipe introduction)
1 tsp rose water, or orange blossom water (optional)
½ tsp ground cardamom and/or ground cinnamon
grating of nutmeg
250ml plant-based milk, organic dairy milk, or water

Blend everything together until smooth. Pour into a saucepan and gently warm through until steamy.

Pour into a mug, cradle and sip.

HOLY BASIL CHAI

Sweet and aniseedy, with natural hints of cinnamon, holy basil is not only delicious, it's also emerging as a wonder herb in scientific studies. Nicknamed the 'queen of herbs', it's known more formally as tulsi. One of its most alluring attributes, beyond taste, is a bestowing of the gift of calm. Drinking it makes you feel serene and that's because it has a positive effect on your stress glands (adrenals). It's a great swap for coffee if you're trying to cut down. Free from caffeine, it can be sipped at any time of day.

SERVES 1

1 tbsp dried holy basil leaves
½ tsp ground cinnamon, or Masala chai (see page 231)
a few twists of freshly ground black pepper, or 4 lightly
    crushed peppercorns
2–3 slices of root ginger
250ml freshly boiled water

Bundle the holy basil leaves and spices into a teapot and pour over the measured boiling water. Steep for 5 minutes, then strain and drink.

STEAMY DANDELION OAT LATTE

Dandelion root has the most incredibly smoky, coffee-like flavour notes. You can either forage the roots from your own garden or buy them (in root or powder form) online or in health food shops. Bundling up for a winter walk to gather your own is not only a brilliant way of getting some fresh air in the dormant months, but freshly gathered roots also offer the richest flavour.

The root is a brilliant source of antioxidants, vitamins A and C and minerals, including potassium and zinc. Such rich, vital nutrition helps us to be more resilient to stress and this drink is a great caffeine-free alternative to coffee.

SERVES 2

For the dandelion root
fresh raw foraged dandelion roots, or 2 tbsp ground dandelion root
    (see recipe introduction)

For the rest
250ml freshly boiled water
½ tsp ground cinnamon
250ml oat milk

If you are starting with the raw roots, preheat the oven to 160°C/150°C fan. You will first need to soak the raw roots in fresh water to remove any soil, then give them a good scrub. Chop the roots into small pieces.

Roast the raw roots, if using, for 45–60 minutes, or until they have thoroughly dried, turned dark brown and give off a rich coffee-like aroma. Remove from the oven and leave to cool.

Grind the root as you would coffee beans.

Add the fresh-roasted or ready-ground root to the measured boiling water in a cafetière with the cinnamon. Brew for 5 minutes.

Warm the oak milk in a saucepan until steamy.

Pour the dandelion coffee into mugs. Top up with the steamy milk and serve.

INDEX

Stockists directory

ABEL & COLE
Amazing organic winter produce, meat, wild seasonal fish, kefir and store cupboard essentials delivered to your door.
abelandcole.co.uk

FOOD FOR ALL
Gorgeous non-profit health online (and in-person) food store with an enormous range of herbs, spices, booster powders, seeds, nuts and dried fruits.
foodforall.co.uk

G BALDWIN & CO
Chinese herbs, mushrooms, medicinal herbs and booster powders.
baldwins.co.uk

GARDEN ORGANIC
Organic seeds and growing advice.
gardenorganic.org.uk

GROWN UP MUSHROOMS
Mushroom growing kits, foraging and growing courses and fresh mushrooms.
grownupmushrooms.co.uk

HALEN MÔN
Sustainable oak woodchips for Chamomile chardonnay (see page 286) and beautiful oak-smoked sea salt for adding woody depth to dishes.
halenmon.com

HAPPY KOMBUCHA
Live cultures to make kombucha and kefir.
happykombucha.co.uk

HODMEDODS
Spectacular range of thoughtfully grown pulses, seeds, flours and grains.
hodmedods.co.uk

HOOK & SON
Brilliant organic, raw dairy (including ghee) from cows reared with love and care, delivered to your door.
hookandson.co.uk

INDIGO HERBS
My go-to brand for booster and wheatgrass powders.
indigo-herbs.co.uk

KOJI KITCHEN
All you need to make homemade miso (see pages 115 and 220).
thekojikitchen.com

NEAL'S YARD REMEDIES
Dried medicinal herbs and wild foods such as dandelion root, elderberries and rosehips, plus products for winter wellness pampering.
nealsyardremedies.com

SKY SPROUTS
The best organic seeds for sprouting and growing nourishing microgreens (see pages 94–95).
skysprouts.co.uk

STEENBERGS
By far – to my mind – the freshest, most flavourful range of spices.
steenbergs.co.uk

TAMARISK FARM
Thoughtfully reared organic beef and lamb, mutton and hogget, as well as barley, rye and heritage wheat.
tamariskfarm.co.uk

THE FERM
Authentic kimchi made by Rebecca Ghim using industry food waste.
thefermlondon.com

TOTALLY WILD UK
Brilliant online plant identification resource.
totallywilduk.co.uk

SOURCES

P76   https://www.sciencedirect.com/science/article/abs/pii/S0304383508003285

P94   https://sphinxsai.com/Vol.3No.4/chem/pdf/CT=25(1886-1890)OD11.pdf

P160   https://www.ncbi.nlm.nih.gov/pmc/articles/PMC8111078/

P278   https://pubmed.ncbi.nlm.nih.gov/23510212/

Acknowledgements

Delivering the manuscript for a book always feels like giving birth, a labour of love with lots of deep breathing and big pushes. As I write this, my incredible editor Lucy Bannell, the diligent and dedicated midwife of *Winter Wellness*, is sweating, probably crying and working overtime as I send over my final bits of copy and textual tweaks. I've worked with so many editors since I studied journalism in the 1990s. Lucy, an ex-Fleet Street pro, truly stands out as one of the best, alongside one of my first editors, Emmy Award-winning Dr Marsha Della-Giustina, who ripped up one of my scripts minutes before I had to deliver it for live television (it taught me resilience). If this book wins any awards, Lucy deserves most of the credit, alongside Sophie Allen, who planted the seed for this book many years ago.

Winter Wellness took a long time to germinate because I had a lot of wintering to do myself after losing the two people I'd known and loved for every winter in my life: my mother Jeannine Stanford and my granddad Loyd Stanford. Their influence shines throughout. I've written this in my first winter without them. Renaissance alchemist Paracelsus said, 'Death is the midwife of very great things...' Nursing me through cloudy days so I could write this is my partner, Stewart Dodd. He and my gorgeous son Rory are the ones I love to share the seasons with most. Now 16, Rory has endured me writing seven books and been an enormous part of the process.

I also have Stewart to thank for introducing me to the team at Bloomsbury Publishing. I've worked with some incredible people in the publishing industry over the past 20 years, but I feel like I've found my home at Bloomsbury. This is my third book with Kitty Stogdon and Rowan Yapp, such a nurturing team who enthusiastically jumped behind this book. Thanks to my agent Claudia Young at Greene & Heaton for perpetuating the process, and Rose Brown and Laura Brodie at Bloomsbury who have been key in giving this book wings. Anna Massardi in publicity and Akua Boateng in marketing are already helping it fly.

When asked who should photograph the book, I instantly thought of Nassima Rothacker. She's well attuned to nature's healing powers. Her wisdom shines through in the stunning images that make this book a work of art. The creative process of bringing the idea of a book to life and making it live up to the fantasy can be challenging and emotional. The results have far exceeded my conceptual dreams. Sandra Zellmer's sagacious skill in sculpting everything together has achieved the peaceful air of calm and beauty I first envisioned.

There have been so many other essential players. At Nassima's studio, we had the wonderful Megan Thomson organising props, Nassima's photography assistants Eyder Rosso, Shashank Verma and Elliya Cleveley, as well as my friends Stéphanie Cruchandeau and Amy Overy for helping me make the recipes look delicious (and washing endless dishes). Enormous thanks, too, to Rebecca Ghim for sharing her kimjang traditions, and to Yuki Gomi. Waka Hasegawa for forever enlightening me with the wonders of Japanese cuisine and Caroline Diggory for healing Polish recipe inspiration. Endless gratitude to nutritional sage Nadia Brydon, who generously shares her wisdom of food's medicinal powers, using it to cure herself of breast cancer.

In the DNA of every book I write are genes stemming from my family, who are all amazing cooks, chefs and gardeners. Some of the most beautiful people I'll ever know are my siblings Robin, Skipper and Marshall and my loving stable of nieces and nephews: you bring immeasurable riches to the world.

I longed to live in the West Country for many years and I'm lucky to have made that dream come true. I'm truly grateful to Hugh Fearnley-Whittingstall for giving me an excuse to plant roots here, and for his and his wife Marie's friendship. I still pinch myself when I walk down the winding path to River Cottage and enormous thanks goes out to the entire team who work tirelessly to make the world of food a healthier and more delicious place.

Tamarisk Farm also deserve high praise, not only for their inspiring and exemplary farming practices, but also for letting Nassima and me turn up on a frosty February morning to take pictures with no forewarning. Tamarisk and River Cottage both feature in the images throughout the book. The rest of the landscape is predominately the place I now call home, a beautiful space to overwinter while writing this book. Finally, my heartfelt thanks go out to you, dear reader, for not only buying the book but engaging with the text. I hope it inspires and nourishes.

RACHEL DE THAMPLE is an award-winning author who has worked in food, health and sustainability for more than twenty years. She teaches fermentation and seasonal nutrition courses at River Cottage in Devon, as well as Petersham Nurseries and the Plant Academy in London. She served as Course Director of the College of Naturopathic Medicine for their Natural Chef diploma, was the Head of Food for the organic retailer Abel & Cole and Commissioning Editor of *Waitrose Food Illustrated*. Rachel has written six books, including *Tonics & Teas* and *Fermentation: River Cottage Handbook No. 18*, which won a Guild of Food Writers Award. She's also studied sustainable food systems at University College London and was instrumental in setting up the award-winning Crystal Palace Food Market. Rachel is a contributor to *The Simple Things* and *Where the Leaves Fall* magazines.

Cook's note

In this book, fan oven temperatures are ten degrees Celsius lower than the equivalent conventional oven temperatures. I find this gives the best results.

BLOOMSBURY PUBLISHING
Bloomsbury Publishing Plc
50 Bedford Square,
London, WC1B 3DP, UK
29 Earlsfort Terrace, Dublin 2,
Ireland

BLOOMSBURY, BLOOMSBURY PUBLISHING and the Diana logo are trademarks of Bloomsbury Publishing Plc.

First published in Great Britain in 2023.
Text © Rachel de Thample, 2023.
Photographs © Nassima Rothacker, 2023.

Rachel de Thample and Nassima Rothacker have asserted their right under the Copyright, Designs and Patents Act, 1988, to be identified as Author and Photographer, respectively, of this work.

For legal purposes, the acknowledgements on page 303 constitute an extension of this copyright page.

A catalogue record for this book is available from the British Library.

Library of Congress Cataloguing-in-Publication data has been applied for.

ISBN: HB: 978-1-5266-6687-1;
eBook: 978-1-5266-6688-8;
ePDF: 978-1-5266-6689-5

10 9 8 7 6 5 4 3 2 1

Project Editor: Lucy Bannell
Designer: Sandra Zellmer
Photographer: Nassima Rothacker
Prop Stylists: Megan Thomson and Rachel de Thample
Food Stylist: Rachel de Thample
Indexer: Vanessa Bird

Printed and bound in Germany by Mohn Media.

MIX
Paper | Supporting responsible forestry
FSC® C011124
www.fsc.org

To find out more about our authors and books, visit www.bloomsbury.com and sign up for our newsletters.